BUILDING BETTER ADS

New Home Advertising That Works

Fourth Edition

Richard L. Elkman

HOME
BUILDER
PRESS

A Service of

NAHB

Home Builder Press®
National Association of Home Builders
1201 15th Street, NW
Washington, DC 20005-2800

Building Better Ads: New Home Advertising That Works
Fourth Edition
ISBN 0-86718-418-3
Copyright © 1996 by Home Builder Press®
National Association of Home Builders of the United States

Cover by Bob DiStefano, Group Two Advertising, Philadelphia.
Printed in the United States of America.

Library of Congress Cataloging in Publication Data

Elkman, Richard L.
　　Building better ads: new home advertising that works/Richard L.
Elkman.
　　　　p.　cm.
　　ISBN　0-86718-418-3
　　1. Advertising–Real estate business. I. Title.
　　HF6161.R3E45　1996　　　　　　　　　　　　　　　96-21824
　　659.1'933333–dc20　　　　　　　　　　　　　　　　CIP

Disclaimer
This publication is designed to provide accurate and authoritative information in regard to the subject matter covered. It is sold with the understanding that the publisher is not engaged in rendering legal, accounting, or other professional service. If legal advice or other expert assistance is required, the service of a competent professional person should be sought.

　– From a Declaration of Principles jointly adopted by a Committee of the
　　American Bar Association and a Committee of Publishers and
　　Associations

For further information, please contact:
　Home Builder Press®
　1201 15th Street, NW, Washington, DC 20005-2800
　(800) 223-2665

CONTENTS

FIGURES

$\mathscr{A}$DVERTISE (ad-ver-tise) *vb* **-tised; tising a:** to make something generally known or to notify especially by a printed notice or a broadcast; **b:** to call public attention to a product or service, especially by emphasizing desirable qualities and so cause a desire to buy or patronize; **c:** to focus on marketing goals and/or to support sales efforts through motivation and enticement.

Please note that nowhere in this definition does it say "advertising sells."
Advertising entices, informs, motivates–but does not sell.

ABOUT THE AUTHOR

Richard L. Elkman, president of Group Two Advertising, started the real estate marketing and advertising company in Philadelphia in 1970. Since then, Group Two has helped both large and small companies in the building industry grow and prosper. It currently operates in 20 states and Canada and represents more than 350 communities. These clients have annual sales in excess of $1.3 billion a year.

Group Two has won numerous national, regional, and local real estate marketing and advertising awards. Elkman has been an active participant and speaker at the NAHB Convention, the Multi-Housing World Info-Expo, Lee Evans' Presidential Seminar, the Pacific Coast Builders Conference, the Builder 100 Conference, as well as regional and local seminars.

Elkman is past president of the Institute of Residential Marketing, a member of the Urban Land Institute, a former Sales and Marketing Council Trustee, and was a master of ceremonies for NAHB's Sales and Marketing Council Awards.

He is the author of three previous editions of this publication, *Classified Information, Building Better Ads*, and *Real Estate Advertising: Problems, Solutions, Results*, and of *Radio Commercials That Work for the Building Industry*, an audiotape package that is now out of print. His articles on real estate advertising have appeared in almost every housing publication across the country.

Elkman received his Bachelor of Arts degree in graphic design from Carnegie-Mellon University in Pittsburgh in 1965.

Acknowledgments

The author wishes to thank Cambridge Homes, Crosswinds Communities, Duffy Homes, Fox Ridge Homes, Kettler Forlines, Macom Corporation, Snyder Hunt Realty, Toll Brothers, Washington Homes, Wayne Homes, and Westminster Homes. Their stories are featured in the Advertising Success Story portion of this book. Thanks go out to all the clients who appear throughout the pages of this book, including Blenheim Homes; Gale, Wentworth, and Dillon, Inc.; Heritage Club; Himmel; Lindal Cedar Homes; Omega Homes; Rieger Homes; Running Brook Builders; Ryland; Sharbell; and The Value Group. The ads appearing in the Problems, Solutions, Results section were recipients of the National Sales and Marketing Awards sponsored by the National Association of Home Builders. The author also wishes to thank several Group Two employees, including Bobbi Helms, Vice President/Creative Director; Bob DiStefano, Vice President/Senior Art Director; Lisa O'Donnell, Senior Copywriter; and Kim Crater, Administrative Art Director, for their contributions.

Reviewers

The following people reviewed the outline and/or the manuscript for this book: Lyda Akin, Vice President, Account Services, Hay Agency, Dallas, Texas; Barbara Cruz, CRB, CRS, President, Jay Cruz Development, Corpus Christi, Texas; Rhonda Daniels, Director, NAHB Office of Regulatory Counsel; Roger Fiehn, MIRM, President, Roger Fiehn and Associates, Houston, Texas; Sue Hawkes, MIRM, Principal, Hawkes and Associates, Woburn, Massachusetts; Meg Meyer, Executive Director, NAHB Sales and Marketing Council; Terri Monrad, Associate Publisher,

New Homes, Overland Park, Kansas; Robert L. Osborn, Coowner, America's Choice Homes, Inc., Norman, Oklahoma; Fred Parker, President, Fred Parker Company, Inc., Fort Worth, Texas; E. Lee Reid, President, E. Lee Reid and Company, Lake Buena Vista, Florida; Dorie Sulik, MIRM, Director of Builder Marketing, Smythe, Cramer Co., Seven Hills, Ohio; and B. J. Young, MIRM, MRA, CRE, President/Owner, B. J. Young, Inc., Winter Park, Florida.

Book Production

This completely revised fourth edition of *Building Better Ads: New Home Advertising That Works* was produced under the general direction of Kent Colton, NAHB Executive Vice President/CEO, in association with NAHB staff members Jim Delizia, Staff Vice President, Member and Association Relations; Adrienne Ash, Assistant Staff Vice President, Publishing and Information Services; Rosanne O'Connor, Director of Publications; Doris M. Tennyson, Director Special Projects/Senior Editor and Project Editor; David Rhodes, Art Director; Kirby Crum, Marketing Director and Carolyn Kamara, Editorial Assistant.

$\mathcal{I}$NTRODUCTION

$\mathcal{O}$pening any newspaper to the real estate section shows just why builders need a competitive edge in the housing industry today. Often a dozen builders or more–large and small–are competing for the same prospective buyers. (In large metropolitan areas, the numbers of competing builders can range much higher.) No matter how good a builder's product, location, and prices are, the homes will not sell unless people know about them.

Newspapers are likely to be a builder's primary source of advertising because newspapers generally are the most cost-effective way to reach the people who will buy the builder's homes. The newspaper real estate section is usually the first place prospective home buyers and area brokers look to see what is available. In newspaper ads the builder can show the product, tell a story, and carve a niche for his or her homes or development that no other home builder can match.

This book is designed to help builders create more effective newspaper ads. However, many of these ads can be used in other media as well, including local magazines, relocation guides, and other publications. The examples included here feature eye-catching graphics and unusual head-lines. All advertising, whether it be for cat food, pickup trucks, or soft drinks, must first catch the attention of the readers and draw them into the ad for more information. But an effective ad does not stop there. Almost any talented writer and artist can create an ad that will attract attention. A successful ad, one that will deliver traffic to your sales office, must do more. It must motivate the reader to pick up the phone and call or–more importantly–visit your site. The ad must offer the reader some kind of benefit. Otherwise the reader will pass over the ad and turn the page. You will lose the opportunity to turn this prospect into a buyer.

If builders study these ads, they can learn from them. As different as the style, location, and price of the homes advertised may be, each ad has successfully delivered qualified traffic, under widely varied market conditions, to developments throughout the country.

This book is a step-by-step guide for both large- and small-volume builders and remodelers. It illustrates the most effective real estate advertising strategies for sales of single-family, multifamily, and custom homes in both large and small markets. This workbook of ideas is based on sound marketing strategies. It presents the Advertising Requirements of the Fair Housing Act and shows how to comply with the Requirements. A competitive edge may be just a few pages away.
This book will help builders find it.

Richard L. Elkman

CHAPTER ONE

STRATEGY
Target Marketing

*A*dvertising is most effective when it is directed to a known target market, rather than an ill-defined one. Therefore success in real estate advertising depends on the builder's ability to determine who the buyer is and what his or her expectations are. Market research, whether handled within the builder's own organization or by a professional market research firm, is the best way to avoid creating ads (and communities) that are inappropriate for the target market.

How do builders go about assembling the data essential to target their marketplace? First, builders must define the target market and identify the types of target markets they can expect to find.

Generally age, sex, socioeconomic factors (demographics), and lifestyle (psychographics) are the criteria used to break down the broad market into smaller segments called target markets. The target market simply refers to that part of the population most likely to buy the builder's homes. Usually, builders have five primary target markets: first-time, move-up, luxury, singles-couples, and empty nesters. Research conducted by *Builder* magazine in its annual Home Buyer Survey revealed the following insights into these five main buyer groups.[1]

First-Time Buyers

This group is possibly the most diverse of all buyer groups. In it you'll find young couples (both with and without children) single people, and divorced people. Today's entry-level home buyers are generally older and more ethnically and demographically different from those in the past. They also have more money to spend and are more careful how they spend it. Most choose to become owners for financial reasons: to get tax breaks and build equity. Many first-time buyers are realistic about what they can afford, so skip the fluff, and just give them high quality and the facts (Figure 1-1).

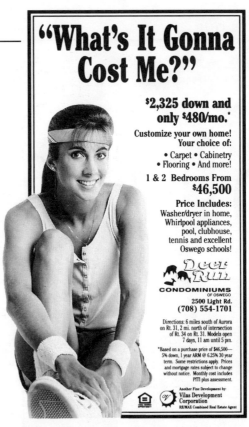

Figure 1-1. Price-conscious first-time buyers want facts and figures. Actual ad size, 4.25" x 7".

Figure 1-2. Photographs of children catch the eye of move-up buyers. Actual ad size, 6.5" x 10".

Move-Up Buyers

This buyer segment consists primarily of families who are looking for a larger, higher-quality home and amenities. For most of them, parenthood is the major motivation to move up. Getting them to "move out"–that is, to expand their home shopping base rather than limit it to strictly nearby or well-established areas can be tough. Most want to avoid severing ties with familiar faces such as friends, pediatricians, and babysitters. However you can tempt them with better schools, better neighborhoods, better amenities–better anything (Figure 1-2).

Luxury Buyers

Free from the financial constraints that force other buyers to make compromises, luxury buyers want– and are willing to pay for–all the extras, upgrades, and top-quality details that add to the price and the value of these homes. For this small but growing market, home is usually filled with luxury features and highly customized. It is also a showplace for entertaining business associates and clients, so the home must convey the message of status loud and clear.

Figure 1-4. Show singles/couples how much better their lives will be in your homes or community. Actual ad size, 13" x 21".

While space is important, it must be comfortable, not overwhelming. These privileged buyers also want large lots and a prestigious location that is close to work (Figure 1-3).

Singles/Couples

This buyer market is more diverse than its name suggests. It includes married couples without children; those never married, divorced, or widowed and living alone; and unrelated people sharing the same living quarters. Singles/couples want open floorplans and a house that reflects their individuality and character.

They are generally willing to sacrifice space for more features–but insist upon lots of light and landscaped views. Committed to career, singles/couples are attracted to low-maintenance living and, like many first-time home buyers, their primary reason for house hunting is financial: to enjoy tax breaks and build equity. Resale value is critical to this target market group who, more than any other entry-level buyers, view a first home as a stepping stone (Figure 1-4).

Empty Nesters

Once a part of the singles/couples target market, the empty nester segment has been growing so fast that marketers now consider it to be a separate buyer group. The childless, mature home buyer's "wish list" includes many of the same wants and desires expressed by singles/couples. Empty nesters tend to favor low-maintenance home designs, open floor plans for entertaining, and modest upgrades that set a house apart. Interiors with first-floor master bedroom suites and two-car garages with easy access to the kitchen are a plus. Typically the most neglected of all buyer groups, the empty nester market is reported to be the fastest growing segment of the population. According to the NAHB Economics Department, more than 10,000 people are turning 50 per day. Builders would be wise to start listening (Figure 1-5).

Identification of the target market begins the moment a builder pinpoints a piece of land. At this time, the location must be clearly examined to determine immigration and outmigration, population trends, employment figures, and per capita income. These statistics will indicate the economic feasibility of the community by revealing the types of services and recreational, cultural and employment opportunities available. Once the builder obtains this information, identifying the types, sizes, and prices of housing that are needed becomes easier.

For example, if the surrounding population is primarily over 55 years of age, married or widowed with no children living at home, and retired, people are more likely to need a two- to three-bedroom, low-maintenance townhome or single-family home. The poplulation would have little need for a four-bedroom, single-family home.

By skillfully defining and understanding the marketplace, a builder can avoid developing homes and communities that no one wants or needs.

Buyer Profiles-Hitting the "Hot Buttons"

Once the builder has firmly established the demand, the builder's advertising agency is ready to create an

Figure 1-5. Over 55 doesn't mean old age anymore. Actual ad size, 6.5" x 11".

advertising campaign that attracts and keeps the target market's attention. To do this, the agency must, once again, call upon market research. (For information about how and when to hire an advertising agency, turn to page 10.)

Although the ad agency is not typically responsible for compiling research, it does assist in its interpretation. The builder's ad agency will study research findings to devise a profile of the targeted buyer based on buyers' lifestyle choices (what they buy, where they work, how they spend their leisure time). Understanding how buyers are going to use their homes and how they live often governs the advertising approach taken. For example, luxury buyers like a prestigious location, and good schools are a top priority for move-up buyers. This type of information helps the creative people to use hot-button words and phrases that will move prospects into action.

Hot buttons can be words and phrases associated with the target market's lifestyle or the actual features and amenities they crave (Figure 1-6).

Builders should use these lifestyle choices, and the hot buttons that convey this information, whenever possible, especially in the merchandising of model homes; in sales office displays; brochures and collateral; and most definitely in advertising.

The more easily buyers can see themselves in a builder's home or community, the greater the chance that these prospects will visit the site. While words can help paint a picture of how much someone's life will improve by moving to a home or community, nothing replaces the impact of pictures. Photographic images are usually the strongest, but newspaper reproduction is often a hit-or-miss situation. Realistic drawings, which almost always reproduce well, can also be quite effective. With the advent of user-friendly computer graphics programs and electronic clip art libraries, even those builders on the most limited budgets can usually afford to add an illustration to their ads.

When directing an ad to a specific target market, you must pay particular attention to avoid stereotyping potential buyers. Certain words, phrases, or images can appear demeaning, rude, biased, or sexist. (For examples of how to avoid this situation or problem, see Chapter 4.)

The Advantage of Positioning

Positioning deals with how to make a particular builder's homes, communities, or company stand out from the competition. A builder must develop a position, or create a niche, in order to attract qualified buyers. The bottom line? The more qualified prospects who visit a site, the greater the percentage of sales.

What is your first step in developing a position? You must start by checking out the competition:

- Read the local papers.
- Shop neighboring communities.
- Talk to brokers.
- Find out who's building what, where, and why.
- Compare not only square footage, but also features, options, and upgrades.
- Most important, find out if they are selling homes.

Figure 1-6. "Hot Buttons"

First-time buyers want value.
- "Stop renting…start building equity now!"
- "Get more home for your money."
- "Get all the "extras"…at no extra charge."
- Walk-in closets
- Built-in microwave oven

Move-up buyers think family and flexibility.
- "Expandable floorplans grow as you grow."
- "Kids attend award-winning schools!"
- "Bonus space makes a great home office or play room!"
- Spacious eat-in kitchen
- Fabulous on-site recreation

Luxury buyers want status and individuality.
- "You deserve to live this well!"
- "Customize from a variety of deluxe options and upgrades…"
- Opulent master bedroom suites
- Dramatic entry foyers
- Prestigious address

Singles-couples want style.
- "Entertain with pride…"
- "You select finishing choices"
- "Great resale value!"
- Formal and informal living areas
- Top quality brand name features

Empty nesters want easy living.
- "Enjoy a spectacular maintenance-free lifestyle!"
- "Easy access to family and friends!"
- First-floor master suite
- Attached two-car garage
- Open, airy designs

This information is invaluable in developing both product and position. It can often make the difference between success and failure.

Once you have insight into what the competition is doing in terms of both product and advertising, you need to start planning. Whether you are planning to build only a few homes or an entire community, you and your team should establish certain goals. These goals include design, price, marketing strategy, and advertising criteria. In other words, how to position the product to make it different (real or perceived) from the competition. And at the same time, you need to keep the target market in sight.

One of the most difficult parts of the positioning process for many builders is being honest with themselves about the kinds of homes and/or communities they are building. They must resist the temptation to build homes they want to build rather than homes buyers want to buy. Failure to do so will not only waste time, energy, and advertising dollars, it will also put builders out of business.

Many builders use the figure of 1 to 2 percent of projected annual sales to determine their advertising budget. But markets and conditions vary. Your budget needs to be flexible enough to withstand rapidly changing market conditions. The size and message of your ads may need to be adjusted to reflect these changes. And, the ads must reach the target market frequently enough to motivate the prospects to visit.

A better method for determining how much money to spend on advertising is to establish realistic sales goals by month and year. Through historical data, research, and "guesstimate," you can determine your closing ratio (that is, the total number of qualified prospects needed to sell one home). After you determine the closing ratio, multiply the closing ratio by your desired sales goal. This figure represents the number of prospects needed to visit the community monthly and annually in order to give the salespeople the opportunity to reach projected sales goals. For example, if 1 out of every 10 prospects who visit your sales center buys 1 of your homes, and your goal is to sell 10 homes in a year, then you need 100 prospects to meet your goal.

Remember, the role of advertising is to bring qualified prospects to the sales environment. Your salespeople are responsible for the actual selling.

Change and Flexibility

Builders must be willing to occasionally modify their advertising, not only to stay fresh and creative, but also to keep up with the competition. Flexibility is often the difference between survival and success. Those builders who stay attuned to changes in their markets and in the world around them, and who are able to respond quickly to those changes, historically

Figure 1-7. *Promotional offers attract attention and add urgency to your message. Actual ad size, 7.5" x 12.75".*

are more successful than others.

Consider: a prospective homebuyer opens the real estate section of the newspaper and sees two ads. Community one's ad is promotional (that is, it highlights a specific sales and/or seasonal event). It focuses on limited-time savings during a Columbus Day sale. Community two's ad is more generic in nature with no special offer and little or no sense of urgency to draw attention to it (Figure 1-7) . Guess which community draws the most traffic that week?

Creativity is the last legal way to gain an unfair advantage over your competition. Being an advertising trendsetter will usually attract attention and qualified traffic to a community. An ad that looks different will almost always get noticed first.

But you also must be prepared to do what other builders are doing occasionally.

For example, if most builders in the market are running promotional ads, a nonpromotional ad will most likely be overlooked. However an ad concept from one builder should not be copied by another. Rather, you need to create just as much excitement in your promotional ads. You could offer special options or upgrade packages instead of lowering prices. Unless the homes or communities are in a distressed situation, you should never devalue your homes.

Your ads also don't have to be as big as your competition's ads. Just be sure your advertising is creative, attracts attention, and conveys a sense of urgency and excitement. Bigger isn't always better. Similarly, creativity alone, with no thought given to the builder's target market, is no guarantee of success either.

Look at real estate ads from other markets. Some publications with excellent real estate sections include the *Newark Star Ledger, Fort Lauderdale Sun Sentinel, Chicago Tribune, Washington Post, Los Angeles Times, Philadelphia Inquirer, Boston Globe, Denver Post,* and *Houston Chronicle.*

Often, ideas translate well from one section of the country to another. While you do not want to copy someone's art and/or words, no law says builders cannot use someone else's idea as a starting point for their own ads. In other words, you could use the basic idea of a promotion but not the exact wording or artwork.

For examples of promotional or seasonal advertising, look to the retail advertising sections of the paper. Sales and events occur in connection with every major (and many minor) holidays. But don't stop there. Be creative. As long as you adhere to the basic tenets of good taste, almost anything goes. Tie an event into something that is happening in the community, the weather, the time of year, whatever (Figure 1-8).

Figure 1-8. Promotional ads can tie into local or national news events. Actual ad size, 10.25" x 18".

9

How to Choose an Advertising Agency

Effective advertising takes an exceptional working relationship between client and advertising agency. Before hiring an agency, builders must answer the following questions:

- How long has the agency been in business?
- Can the agency provide a list of client references?
- Does the agency have experience with new home advertising?
- What are the agency's capabilities?
- What billing policies does the agency use?

How Long Has the Agency Been in Business?

Whether you hire a new, small advertising agency or a large one that has been in business for many years, you should find out as much as possible about the financial stability of the company.

Can the Agency Provide a List of Client References?

Claims can often be misleading. You need to know how the advertising agency interacts with client personnel, what billing policy they use, how quickly work is processed and how they monitor results and adjust to changes. This information can only be given by former clients. Finding out about an agency before signing a contract can prevent the waste of both time and money.

What Is the Advertising Agency's Marketing Philosophy?

The philosophies of the personnel at the agency who will be working on the builder's behalf must match the builder's in order to develop a well-directed business plan. If the builder and the creative team are at odds with one another, a cohesive, consistent campaign is less likely to result.

Does the Agency Have Experience with New Home Advertising?

Why should you spend time and money to educate an advertising agency about the housing industry? If a local or regional advertising agency has housing experience, using it may be cost-efficient. If you narrow the choice to more than one agency experienced in the housing industry, why not select one that is involved in such organizations as the National Association of Home Builders, the National Sales and Marketing Council, or other local and state building organizations?

What Are the Agency's Capabilities?

You should make certain that the same people who created the advertising in the agency's portfolio will work on your account. If most of the portfolio was created by the people who are no longer with the agency or if the agency is planning to turn your work over to new people or interns, you may want to reconsider. You may also want to meet with the agency's creative people to see if you are comfortable with them.

What Billing Policies Does the Agency Use?

Agencies bill clients in several different ways. Some charge 15 percent or 17.65 percent of the media costs as a service fee. Others work by keeping the commissions from the media. Still others negotiate a monthly fee or retainer. Agencies also have different billing rates for creative services such as writing copy, doing the layout, and preparing the mechanical paste-up (material given to a printer that is ready for printing). As builders, periodicals, and advertising agencies use more disks and electronic files, use of mechanical paste-ups is on the decline.

Some agencies mark up out-of-pocket expenses (such as typesetting, photostats, and illustrations). These mark-ups generally range from 15 to 20 percent. Comparing these costs is a vital part of selecting an new advertising agency. Understanding form the beginning how the agency is going to charge for its services prevents misunderstandings in the future.

CHAPTER TWO

THE WRITE STUFF
Benefits and Features

*A*ll successful advertising offers some kind of benefit to motivate prospects to call or visit the community. Notice the word *benefit* not feature. They are different. A feature is a tangible item that is built-in or comes with the home when you buy it. A benefit is the value a prospect can expect to gain from that particular feature. For example, vinyl siding is a feature, but never having to paint your house is a benefit.

The first step in writing ads that sell is to write about benefits not features. If possible, offer benefits that no other builders are offering or mentioning in their ads. Coming up with distinctive benefits can be difficult, but dig deep. A strong knowledge of the product and of your competition's will reveal what makes your homes different, and therefore better than the rest.

Remember, people don't just buy homes as shelter. They buy what those homes can offer them. Target the prospect's wants and needs. If an ad answers the question, "What's in it for me?" it will surely attract attention.

Typically builders think from a construction perspective, rather than a marketing one. Therefore they are tempted to list technical features that have little or no meaning to the consumer. Highlight just a few of the homes' or communities' many benefits. Give the prospects too much information, and they may decide they have no need to visit. Instead, use reader-friendly words or terms that paint a picture for the readers and whet their appetites to call or visit for more information.

Headline Dos and Don'ts

No matter how much time and energy you put into the creation of an ad, many prospective buyers will only scan it. They will note the headline, the name of the community, the price, and the illustration or photograph. Only if readers are intrigued will they read more.

The headline and primary graphic of an ad are its two most important elements. The most effective headlines are those that address the target market, especially in classified advertising (Figures 2-1A, 2-1B, and 2-1C). The headline must grab the eye of the reader quickly.

The most effective headlines –
- are short but manage to deliver a complete message
- target the audience
- grab the reader's attention
- use strong, powerful words such as *free*, *new*, *save*, *first*, and *great*
- draw the reader into the body copy
- offer a benefit
- are tied into the visual

(Figures 2-2, 2-3, 2-4 and 2-5)

Ineffective headlines–
- are too long to read quickly
- talk down to the target market
- are offensive
- are confusing
- do not offer any benefit to the reader
- do not relate to the visual

Are there exceptions to these rules? Of course some successful ads have featured long headlines. But most of these ads had little or no body copy. Essentially, the headline was the ad copy (Figure 2-6).

Rip Us Off!

Mention this ad when you visit and get a **FREE washer and dryer** when you buy a new home at

The Woodlands
From $99,900

| • 2 & 3 BR townhomes | • Close to shopping | • Ask about our move-in |
| • Fireplaces included | • Swimming, tennis, more! | special |

1234 Mason Blvd. • 1 block north of 12th Street • 345-5677

A

WILD NEIGHBORS!

Beautiful wooded setting with squirrels, rabbits, birds galore!

- 2 & 3 BR townhomes
- Fireplaces included
- Close to shopping
- Swimming, tennis, more!
- Ask about our move-in special

The Woodlands
From $99,900

1234 Mason Blvd. • 1 block north of 12th Street 345-5677

B

LIVE FREE!

We'll pay your first month's mortgage payment!

- 2 & 3 BR townhomes
- Fireplaces included
- Close to shopping
- Swimming, tennis, more!
- Ask about our move-in special

The Woodlands
From $99,900

1234 Mason Blvd. • 1 block north of 12th Street 345-5677

C

Figures 2-1.
Focus on creative words and phrases to catch attention in classified display ads if your newspaper will allow ads like these. Actual ad sizes, 4" x 3.5".

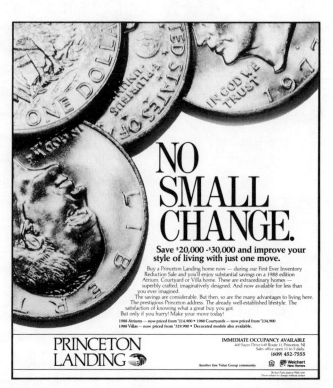

Figure 2-2. This creative headline makes perfect "cents." Actual ad size, 9.75" x 11".

Figure 2-3. Listen to the words and phrases your buyers use. You might be able to turn them into effective headlines. Actual ad size, 4.75″ x 10″.

Figure 2-4. This ad uses a successful variation on a popular theme. Actual ad size, 6.5″ x 10.5″

Throw your money away.

(Buy someone else's home.)

You always get more in an Omega home.

Visit any Omega community and tour our homes. You'll discover what our family of Lehigh Valley homeowners already has. No one delivers more quality, value or service.

We dedicate ourselves to building excellence into every detail of our homes and communities.

From our wide array of "standard extras" that are included in every home, to our imaginative use of space and light, it's easy to see we offer a better home at a better price.

Whatever you're looking for in a new home and a new neighborhood, look for our name.

Because if you don't, you're just throwing your money away.

ΩMEGA HOMES
QUALITY • VALUE • SERVICE

PENN'S GRANT — **GRAND OPENING!** Priced from $87,900.
Directions: Take Rt. 22 to 25th St. Exit. Take Rt. 248 West to Park Ave. & turn right at Palmer Park Mall. Proceed past mall & continue to Tatamy Rd. Follow signs to Sales Office 1.5 miles on the right. Open Mon. & Thurs. 1-6, Fri. - Sun. 1-5. Other hours by appt. FHA approved. (610) 515-1355

BORO PARK — **ONLY 6 REMAIN!** Single family homes from $129,900
Directions: From Rt. 22, take Rt. 145 N. to stoplight at Rt. 329. Turn right onto 329 E. Go over bridge and turn left at stoplight onto Main St. in Northampton. Continue to next light and turn left onto Cherryville Rd. Pass shopping center and turn right on 30th St. Office/model is first house on the right. Open Mon. and Fri. 12-5, Thurs. 12-6, Sat. & Sun. 1-5. Tues & Wed. by appt. (610) 262-2900

BORO VIEW NORTHAMPTON — **PRE-CONSTRUCTION PRICES!** Priced from $105,000
Directions: Please follow directions for Boro Park shown above. Open Mon. and Fri. 12-5, Thurs. 12-6, Sat. & Sun. 1-5. Tues. & Wed. by appt. (610) 262-2900

Figure 2-5. Throw away the book on writing headlines. Breaking rules is allowed and encouraged. Actual ad size, 6.75" x 9.5".

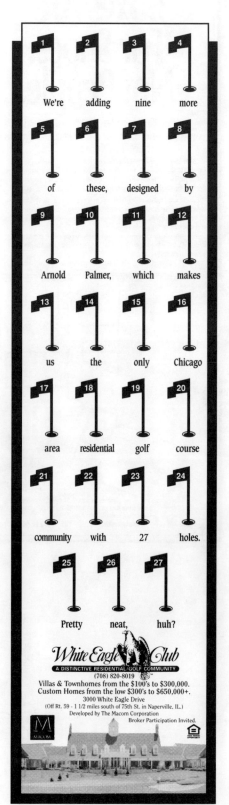

Figure 2-6. This unique ad was on par with some of the best. Actual ad size, 4.25" x 15.75".

Body Copy Basics

One way to encourage prospective buyers to read the body copy is to make it easy to read. Keep it short. Keep it simple. Use "picture" words whenever possible (words that elicit pleasant memories and positive emotional responses) (Figure 2-7).

You don't need to list every feature of your home or community in one ad; you want to keep the prospects interested. Concentrate on those features that the competition does not offer or charges extra for. In other words, let your prospects know what is different and better about your homes and community. Give them a reason to visit and to buy now versus later.

Depending upon the size of the ad, it is often better to bullet copy points, than to write them in sentence form. This format is easy to scan and works perfectly for those just glancing through the real estate section (Figure 2-8).

Figure 2-7. Paint a picture in words and phrases that will make your buyers feel at home. Actual ad size, 5.75" x 10".

Figure 2-8. Bullet copy to make it easy to read and remember. Actual ad size, 3.75" x 3.25".

If space allows, bulleted copy points should still convey benefits rather than just features.

In advertising, choosing the right word is essential in order to attract the reader's attention. Avoid using terms that discriminate or just plain bore the reader. What follows is a list of words common to the home building industry and their better, more consumer friendly alternatives.

Avoid	Replace It With
• lot	homesite
• house	home
• cheap	affordable or attractively priced
• development	neighborhood or community
• established	well-known and/or desirable address
• private	secluded

When writing body copy–

Don't Offend–Humor can be effective, but proceed with caution. Make sure it suits the subject and/or situation. Using it inappropriately can decrease credibility and alienate potential buyers.

Don't Exclude the Reader–Use the words *you* and *your* frequently and treat potential buyers in a friendly way rather than as an outsider.

Don't Mislead–If you dare the reader to compare your home or community to the competition, you must include facts to support the claim. Unsubstantiated claims breed skeptical buyers. Resist any temptation to distort the facts (Figure 2-9).

Figure 2-9. Be honest with your buyers. Include only the features or benefits your houses have. Actual ad size, 10.75" x 8.5".

Mandatory Items

The most effective ads are the ones that tell a simple story, not ones jammed with facts and figures. Many builders feel obligated to fill up every inch of ad space– a mistake. White space or blank space makes an ad easier to read and more attractive. Too much information becomes too much work for a prospect to muddle through; therefore, the builder must be selective. The paragraphs below discuss the mandatory elements that you should include in every ad (Figures 2-10A and 2-10B).

Price–First-time buyers and young professionals are particularly price sensitive. Some builders may ask whether to list a price range or a specific price. Generally, when the price spread is narrow (for example, 15 percent or less), you would list the starting price. Listing a price range works better when the variation in price is greater than 15 percent. Because price is a qualifier, it must be in the ad in order to attract qualified traffic, not just lookers, to the site.

Phone Number–An ad may attract the buyer's attention, but it won't do any good unless it tells the buyer what to do next: call for more information, directions, an appointment, and so forth. Make sure the complete phone number appears on the same line; don't forget to include the area code (especially if your area has more than one code). In terms of point size, the phone number should be at least as large as the body copy.

Directions and/or Map–The ad must tell and/or show prospects how to get to your site. A stick map, a simplified map showing no more than five streets, is often the best way to show prospects the site's location in relation to surrounding major roads and landmarks. If location is a primary selling point, include a stick map

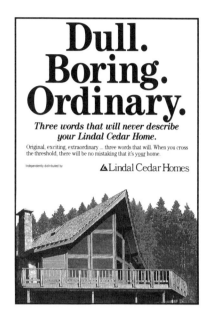

A

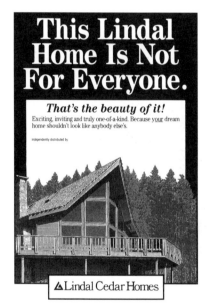

B

Figure 2-10. These ads demonstrate an extraordinary way to catch a buyer's eye in a small space ad. Actual ad size, 2" x 3".

in the ad. Remember to keep written directions, maps, and listings as simple as possible. Make sure the type is large enough to be legible (Figure 2-11).

Equal Housing Logo or Statement– Including this logo is not a suggestion, it's the law. The federal government requires that builders show potential buyers that they comply with the Advertising Requirements of the Fair Housing Act and that they welcome all buyers who can qualify. (See Chapter 4 for a sample of the logo and statement.)

Broker Participation–Invite brokers to bring in clients, and let buyers know that they can work through a broker if they desire. Have registration rules available to give to them so no misunderstandings occur.

Sales Office Hours–Don't risk alienating a potential buyer by having them visit when the sales office is closed. Let buyers know when they can visit and when models are open for viewing. And remember, many prospects are reading the newspaper and looking through brochures after office hours. To avoid missed sales, have an answering service or machine available 24 hours a day.

Warranties and/or Professional Affiliations–These items give prospective buyers information about who you are and how you do business. When space allows, they should be included in your ads.

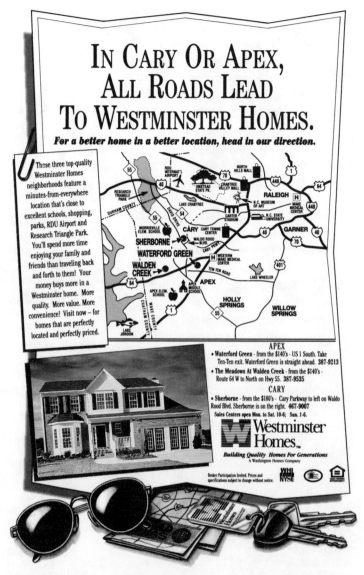

Figure 2-11. Map out the most important information you need to get across. In this ad, location is key. Actual ad size, 6.5" x 10.25".

CHAPTER THREE

GRAB ATTENTION WITH GRAPHICS

Design and Layout

*H*ow an ad looks is as important–or more important–as what it says. If the ad is not appealing to look at, if it doesn't attract attention, it will never be read or acted upon.

You should not assume that just because you use a professional (an advertising agency, graphic design firm, or freelance artist) the ad will be graphically effective for the target market. Give the person who is designing the ad as much market research information as possible. Provide the direction needed to produce the results you want. Remember, the primary purpose of your ad is to attract qualified prospects, not to win awards. When the ad is completed, show it to a group of home buyers and/or homeowners in your target market. See if it attracts their attention.

The following information is provided to help builders know what to look for and what to avoid when designing an ad.

White Space

What is left out of an ad is as important as what is put into it. Leaving white space around the black or colored headline and/or primary graphic helps draw the eye to it. It forms a background that allows the words or artwork to "pop" off the page (Figure 3-1).

You need to resist the urge to fill the ad with words and graphics simply because you are paying for the space. Carefully determine which element should be most prominent.

They cannot all be prominent, nor should they all try to be. Use this simple test to see what attracts the eye most. Turn the ad upside down. The eye will automatically go to the most prominent element of the ad. It should be an important part of the ad message such as the headline or visual–not the sales office hours.

Reversing Out

Large black spaces can be just as eyecatching as large white spaces, especially in small space ads and on real estate pages that are extremely crowded. This effective graphics technique is called reversing out or knocking out the type. In essence, the background of the ad is black (or colored) and the type is white.

A word of warning: don't reverse out large blocks of copy or tiny "mice" size type. It will be unreadable. Script or serif typefaces are also poor choices for reversing out. Uncluttered bold typefaces work best (Figure 3-2).

Snipes, Banners, and Boxes

Adding urgency to an ad gives people a reason to call or visit now, rather than later. One way to draw attention to a limited or special offer is to add a snipe (a thin box filled with a few words of type that usually appears at the top of an ad or a photo) or banner to an existing ad. Place the snipe or banner copy at the top of the ad, across either top corner of the ad, or above the elevation (Figure 3-3).

Never cut into an elevation. You will distort the product. Keep the copy within the banner short. The fewer words used, the larger those words can be. Reversing out the snipe or banner can be quite effective.

Figure 3-1.
Use white space as a graphic element to attract attention. Actual ad size, 6.25" x 10.5".

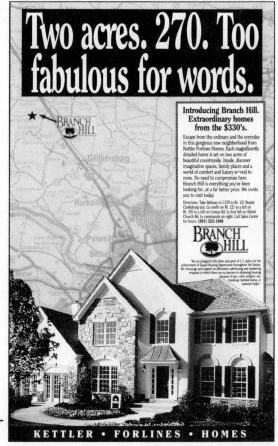

Figure 3-2. Reversing out this headline makes it visually pop off the page. Actual ad size, 6.5" x 10.5".

Figure 3-3. Banners or snipes can be created in almost any shape or size. Actual ad size, 13" x 10.5".

Examples of Snipe or Banner Copy

• "Pre construction Savings!"
• "Free decorating package!"
• "Last 3 homes!"
• "Decorator Model for Sale"
• "Builder closeout–hurry!"
• "Save $10,000 this weekend!"

When the offer or event needs more copy to properly describe it and where space allows, put it into a box (Figure 3-4). Often the copy of an existing ad needs to be cut to make room for this box. But this technique is still less expensive than producing a new ad.

Figure 3-4.Examples of Special Offers Suitable for Boxing

Fall Harvest Festival
1-5 pm, Sunday, Sept. 15
Food! Fun! Music!
Prize Drawings!
Bring the family. Tour our models!

Free washer and dryer!
Buy before October 22 and you'll
get a FREE washer and dryer
as a welcome home present!
Bring this ad with you when you visit.

Offer subject to change without notice.
Only one offer per home

Typeface Selection

Type simply refers to text set in lettering that can be reproduced by a printer. In some large advertising agencies, sometimes an art director does nothing but select the proper typefaces for ads and collateral pieces that other art directors design. While this practice is rare, it does show that the selection of the font, size, and style of type for an ad is an important part of the design process.

Typography

Listed below are some basic rules of typography. Sometimes successful ads break one or more of these rules, but breaking them unknowingly can create serious problems.

Type Size

Headlines should be larger than body copy. Body copy should be larger than disclaimers. Remember, if everything is the same size, nothing will stand out.

Keep the target market in mind. Body copy for active adults or senior citizens needs to be large enough to be read easily, usually no smaller than 11 or 12 point type. Similarly, if the target market is younger–early 20s to 30s–a more contemporary typeface can be used for the headline type.

Keep it simple. Serif typefaces have short lines or "feet" which flair at the upper and lower ends of the strokes of a letter. They are fine for headline type, which tends to have a larger point size, but they make small ads and body copy difficult to read. Generally a serif typeface will become unrecognizable in any type size smaller than 9 point. On the other hand, sans serif typefaces hold up quite well in many type sizes.

Although using several different styles of type in an ad works, it is not wise. Too much variety will only confuse the eye and blur the focus of the ad. Stick to one or two at the most (Figure 3-5).

Figure 3-5. Examples of Typefaces

Serif Typefaces

- This typeface is Century Oldstyle
- This typeface is Clearface
- This typeface is Cheltenham Condensed

San Serif Typefaces

- This typeface is Avant Garde Medium
- This typeface is Geneva
- This typeface is Helvetica Condensed

Use of Photography

Newspapers are remarkably inconsistent when it comes to photographic reproduction quality. One day, all the ads may look great. The next day, half the page is too dark; half is too light. But some techniques can tilt the scale in a builder's favor.

Photographs

If at all possible, use a professional photographer. The adage, you get what you pay for, is true in photography. Also, because of the difference in tonality, have your photographs shot both in black and white and color. Although you can submit a color photograph for a black-and-white ad, it will not reproduce as well.

Similarly, a black-and-white conversion can be made from a color photograph, but again, clarity is lost and the conversion can take 4 to 5 days. Shorter turnaround times are possible–but only with hefty rush charges added. (Some printers now have equipment that can scan directly from color slides, but check with your printer before planning on using color slides for black-and-white ads.)

Halftones and Line Screens

Photographs that appear in ads are called halftones. They are continuous tone images photographed through a line screen to break them up into tiny dots. From normal viewing distance, they appear as continuous shades or tones. Different publications use different line screens. The number assigned to a line screen indicates the number of dots per square inch (dpi). For example, a 65-line screen contains 65 dots per inch, which is the coarsest grain used for black-and-white newspaper reproductions. Some newspapers use 80 and 100 line screens (Figure 3-6). Magazines typically use 130 or 150 line screens for a more refined image. Some direct mail and brochures, on the other hand, use line screens of 200 to 250.

Builders who are sending their photographs directly to the paper need not worry about the line screen. But some builders, and many advertising agencies, send computer scans of the photograph instead. The output of the computer scan must match the newspaper's line screen. Contact the newspaper's production manager for a complete list of their production parameters.

Also check with the manager of the production department of the newspapers you use to see if they have any suggestions for better photographic reproduction. Occasionally, the publications will strip in a half-tone negative shot from a continuous tone print rather than shoot a halftone from a continuous tone print, and then shoot the negative from that. This eliminates one step or generation. The closer a photo is to the original, the clearer and crisper it will be.

Crop the photo for maximum effectiveness-but don't cut off or cover over architectural details of the home. Get as close as possible and make all photographs as large as possible within the ad. However, you need to vary the size of the photographs within an ad. If you make the photographs the same size, nothing will stand out.

The purpose of retouching a photograph is to enhance or subdue details rather than incorporate new details (Figures 3-7 and 3-8). Many art directors have become skilled in the art of retouching photographs on a computer. They can eliminate an overhead power line, add landscaping, turn a gray sky

65 Line Screen Halftone

100 Line Screen Halftone

Figure 3-6. Higher line screens usually produce clearer, crisper photographs. But check with a staff member for each publication before you proceed.

blue. But what they can do is limited, and costs are often prohibitive, as well. Traditional hand retouching is usually less expensive than doing it on a computer. Each method of retouching is time-consuming. Retouching should only be attempted by a professional. If it is not done properly, the results can be embarrassing.

Showing people in a photograph helps the target market identify with a builder's homes and community. Close-ups and action photographs of people are among the most effective. Because some newspapers do not allow photographs of people in real estate advertising, you should check with your local newspapers before spending money on photography.

You can purchase stock photography at per- use or multiple-use rates. Those rates vary depending upon the newspaper's demographics and the market in which the photograph will appear. Taking new photographs is often most cost efficient. Professional models need not be used, but, if at all possible, use a professional photographer.

Regardless of whether you choose to purchase stock photographs or have photographs taken, Fair Housing Requirements must be followed (see Chapter 4). You can contact your local newspapers for the correct percentage of minority representation in their ads. Each newspaper should have a demographic breakdown for its area. In many major markets in the United States, newspapers require a 25 to 33 percent minority representation in ads. Thus, 1 out of every 3 or 4 people pictured in these newspapers' ads must from the minority group.

If a builder chooses not to feature both minority and majority models in the same ad, the ads should be rotated so that at least one-third of the photos feature minority models.

Figure 3-7. Computer retouching deleted a mailbox and a "For Sale" sign from this photograph. Actual ad size, 7.5" x 10".

Figure 3-8. You can find a stock photograph to fit every ad and headline, but keep an eye on the costs. Actual ad size, 7.5" x 9.5".

Border Treatments

One of the most effective ways to separate an ad from those around it, and put forth a consistent image as well, is to create a border treatment. A border works especially well for builders with several communities that are each advertised separately. But even small-volume builders with limited budgets can reap big rewards from the upscale image that a border treatment can convey.

From a simple, thick black line surrounding the ad, to a more intricate and unusual geometric shape that encompasses the builder, name, or community logo, borders are a quick, easy way to make an ad stand out from the competition. Putting the builder or community logo within the border also frees up more space within the ad itself. To create an ad that really stands out, you can use an interesting piece of artwork that actually pops-out of or breaks the border (Figures 3-9, 3-10, and 3-11).

Figure 3-9. A seasonal graphic of leaves forms the left border of this ad. Actual ad size, 6.5" x 10".

Figure 3-10. This entire ad is enclosed in a price tag. Great for first-time buyers. Actual ad size, 3" x 5".

Figure 3-11. A pair of hands holding the ad within a newspaper border really attracts attention. Actual ad size, 7.5" x 10".

CHAPTER FOUR

FAIR HOUSING COMPLIANCE
It's the Law

$\mathcal{M}$any builders and developers do not realize the frequency or seriousness of racial discrimination in real estate advertising. Under federal fair housing law, advertising for prospects based on race, color, nationality, sex, handicap, or familial status is illegal. That rule applies to print, radio, and television advertising, as well as to oral statements made to prospects.[2] Complying with these guidelines is extremely important for every builder, large or small, across the country. An example of complying is including either the Equal Housing Opportunity logo, slogan, or statement in all ads. If using a logo, remember to adhere to the size standards.

If the ad is–

- $^1/_2$ page or larger, the logo must be 2x2 inches
- $^1/_8$ page up to $^1/_2$ page, the logo must be 1x1 inches
- 4 column inches to $^1/_8$ page, the logo must be $^1/_2$ x $^1/_2$ inches
- less than 4 column inches, do not use logotype, use the statement or slogan

EQUAL HOUSING OPPORTUNITY

Figure 4-1. A photograph showing a group of children meets Equal Housing requirements. Actual ad size, 6.5" x 10".

...e advertising, ...ty logo should ... of the other ...portunity slogan ...portunity."[4] The ...sing statement is–

...it of U.S. policy ...g Opportunity throughout the Nation. We encourage and support an affirmative advertising and marketing program in which there are no barriers to obtaining housing because of race, color, religion, sex, handicap, familial status, or national origin.[5]

The use of this logo and/or statement has become common practice in most builders' and developers' advertising. However many do not realize that Equal Housing Requirements also cover the use of models in photographs or illustrations for advertising. This confusion has resulted in serious penalties. Builders, developers, newspapers, and magazines have been sued by the government and fined as much as $2 million for unintentionally discriminating in their advertising (Figures 4-1, 4-2, and 4-3).

In display advertising where human models are used, whether in photographs, drawings, or other graphic renderings, the models should reasonably represent majority and minority racial groups in a way that is clearly definable and numerically representative of the metropolitan area.[6]

According to the regulations issued by the U.S. Department of Housing and Urban Development (HUD), majority and minority representation is a relative term depending on the concentration of the metropolitan area.[7] For example, in regard to ethnic situations, if you are advertising in a primarily Hispanic community, you must include representation of that minority ethnic group in your advertising. In this regard, minority representation in your area might include people of American Indian, African-American, Caucasian, Asian, or Latino descent, among others.

Figures 4-2 and 4-3. Both models were photographed at the same session, saving time and money. Actual ad size, 5" x 7".

In addition, ads should similarly include a reasonable representation of persons of all ages, both sexes, and where applicable, families with children. Models, if used, should portray people in an equal social setting, indicating that the housing is open to all.[8]

Generally, if a third of the models in an ad or a third of the ads feature minorities, the ads should pose no discrimination problems. If you intend to use models in advertisements, plan ahead with photo shoots and/or stock photo selections to adhere to this regulation.

Certain industry "buzzwords"–such as *private, established,* or *exclusive*–are also subject to equal housing requirements, as well as references to geographical landmarks, such as churches or synagogues.

In most cases, discriminatory phrases such as *whites only, no children,* and *Christian home* are clearly understood to be violations. Confusion can arise, however, when seemingly harmless phrases used to describe architectural features or amenities are cited as possible fair housing violations. In a 1995 memo, HUD clarified what words and phrases are not acceptable in real estate advertising.

The checklist in Figure 4-4 includes words and phrases specifically approved in the memorandum: Following the checklist in Figure 4-4 will help you avoid fair housing trouble. But remember, the HUD memorandum applies only to the federal fair housing law. Ads that adhere to HUD guidelines can still be subject to lawsuits filed under state and local fair housing laws. You therefore need to know both the federal regulations and the laws of the state in which you choose to advertise. Perhaps the best advice to follow when questioning the acceptability of certain words or phrases is, when you are in doubt, leave it out.

Figure 4-4. Nondiscriminatory Words and Phrases for Use in Real Estate Advertising

Nondiscrimination Based on Handicap Status
- fourth-floor walk-up
- great view
- jogging trails
- seeking nonsmoking and sober residents
- walk-in closets
- walk to bus stop

Nondiscrimination Based on Religion

Secularized Holiday Terms, Symbols, or Images
- Santa Claus
- Easter Bunny
- St. Valentine's Day
- Merry Christmas
- Happy Easter
- Happy Halloween
- Happy Hanukkah
- Happy Kwanza

General Religious References
- apartment complex with chapel
- kosher meals available

Nondiscrimination Based on Race, Color, National Origin References
- master bedroom
- rare find
- desirable neighborhood

Nondiscrimination Based on Sex Reference
- mother-in-law suite
- bachelor apartment

Nondiscrimination Based on Familial Status
- two bedroom
- cozy
- no bicycles allowed
- quiet streets

Source: U.S. Department of Housing and Urban Development. *Implementation of the Fair Housing Amendments Act of 1988;* 24CRFR Section 109.30, 2-7.

CHAPTER FIVE

ADVERTISING SUCCESS STORIES

A world of difference exists between an ad that just attracts attention and an ad that attracts qualified traffic to a builder's site, as well. What makes these ads so effective can sometimes be found in the message (what it says). Or, it can be found in the graphics (how it looks). But in most cases, the perfect combination of both is what makes the difference. On the following pages are examples of successful ads from builders around the country and the stories behind their creation.

Package Your Message to Make It Stand Out

In *Gypsy*, the Broadway musical about the life of Gypsy Rose Lee, a show-stopping song titled, "You Gotta Have a Gimmick," gives good advice for anyone designing an ad that is to be featured in a crowded section of the newspaper.

Builders and developers spend a great deal of time developing a unique position for their homes and communities. Advertising and marketing materials must communicate this position or message to potential home buyers. If you face competition in the real estate section of the newspaper being used and your prospective home buyers are bombarded with messages, how you deliver the message is as important as what the message says.

The Macom Corporation, developers of White Eagle Club, in suburban Chicago, wanted to announce the fact that they were adding 9 holes to their 18-hole Arnold Palmer Signature golf course. While ads for White Eagle Club regularly appear in community newspapers and lifestyle magazines, the primary advertising medium used is the *Chicago Tribune*.

The *Chicago Tribune* is one of the country's most widely read newspapers. Its real estate section is zoned-divided by geographical locations. This situation is an advantage for a local builder, because an ad can appear only in designated neighborhoods. The builder also saves money by not advertising to the entire *Tribune* readership.

White Eagle Club advertises in the west zoned edition of the *Tribune*. Based on marketing information and direction provided by Paul Lehman, president of Macom Corporation, lifestyle is heavily emphasized in all White Eagle Club ads. And, with more than 500 families already living in this Naperville-Aurora community, this strategy obviously has paid off.

The majority of the ads in the crowded west-zoned edition were of similar size and shape. The advertising agency media director contacted the newspaper to see if it would accept an unusually shaped ad that did not conform to standard ad sizes. The *Tribune* agreed to run the ad, which was designed to be two columns wide by the full length of the page. A preferred right side of the paper was also requested.

Because the primary message of this ad is golf, the entire ad was designed in the shape of a golf bag. Extending from the bag were various golf clubs and a bottle of champagne and two glasses. The headline reads, "We're toasting our success with tee. (Nine to be exact.)"

Body copy was contained within the bag, along with a photograph of the impressive golf clubhouse. This ad easily stood out in the newspaper and attracted the attention of those interested in living in a residential golf community. It also serves as an excellent example. It shows that creativity in advertising is more than just a clever headline and intriguing graphic. Never accept, "it hasn't been done before" as an excuse not to try something new. In White Eagle Club's case, they took their best shot–and won. White Eagle Club is the fastest selling country club community in Chicago (Figure 5-1).

Figures 5-1. This innovative concept produced an attention-getting ad. Actual ad size, 4.25" x 15.75".

We're toasting our success with tee.
(Nine to be exact)

NEW GOLF COURSE HOMESITES AVAILABLE

White Eagle Club will soon be serving up nine new holes of golf on our Arnold Palmer Signature course. (And a superb selection of golf course homesites!) That will make us the only Chicago-area residential golf course community with 27 holes.

White Eagle Club is also home to more than 500 families just like yours. One visit and you'll know why. Our homeowners can choose between a traditional country club lifestyle...or a more casual style of living at the Owners Club.

The distinctive and inviting Owners Club has a zero depth swimming pool, lighted tennis courts, two spas, a sand playground for children with a volleyball area and a clubhouse that's always abuzz with activity.

We invite you to be a part of our success at White Eagle Club in Naperville. Here's to the perfect move for you and your family. Visit now.

White Eagle Club
A DISTINCTIVE RESIDENTIAL/GOLF COMMUNITY

(708) 820-8019

Villas & Townhomes from the $100's to $300,000.
Custom Homes from the low $300's to $650,000+.
3000 White Eagle Drive
(Off Rt. 59 · 1 1/2 miles south of 75th St. in Naperville, IL.)
Developed by The Macom Corporation
Broker Participation Invited.

Hit the "Hot Buttons" of Active Adults

Almost invariably, the more highly targeted an ad, the more effective it is. A real estate ad becomes highly targeted by speaking directly to those who are most likely to buy. Often research reveals what benefits, features, and issues are most important to a specific target market. For example, affordable price and low monthly payments are primary concerns of first-time buyers.

Empty-nester buyers have little or no urgency to move. Builders and developers must provide the motivation to get these people to visit and buy.

Cambridge Homes, one of the largest home builders in Chicago, purchased Carillon, an active adult community in the southwestern suburbs of Chicago. Richard J. Brown, president of Cambridge Homes, decided to convene a focus group study to discover what issues or "hot buttons" appealed most to adults aged 55 and over. Current residents of Cambridge at Carillon were among the participants. Several key words and phrases were mentioned repeatedly during this focus group study, including –

- "friendliness...feeling of community... environment of peers...closeness and compatibility with neighbors... on the same wave length..."
- "emphasis on living...beginning, not ending... social and cultural activities..."
- "townhomes that live like single-family detached homes...price/value... more for the money...maintenance-free living...
  affordable golf course living ..."
- "only adult community in area...A neighborhood like it used to be...no bikes, boomboxes, etc. .. close to grandchildren..."

Interestingly enough, one phrase was so memorable, it formed the basis for the headline of the first new ad, "We're so busy, the kids have to make an appointment to see us."

While a full-page was reserved, only part of space was filled by the ad. An "advertorial" was written to appear above the ad. The "advertorial" is a cross between an ad and an editorial. It looks like a story written by the newspaper–even though the word *advertisement* is typeset at the top. Written by an agency copywriter, it "reported" on the inviting and exciting lifestyle found at Cambridge at Carillon. Future advertorials featured resident testimonials, the opening of the recreation center, and grand openings of new Cambridge at Carillon neighborhoods.

Included in the actual color ad were many of the "hot buttons" uncovered during the focus group study. The words, graphics, and photographs painted a picture showing that everyday life at Cambridge at Carillon was similar to being on vacation 365 days a year.

Copy described the many on-site activities and amenities available in the community–including a public 18-hole golf course and a 32,000-square-foot Recreation Center with theater, crafts, cards, and community rooms and a heated indoor pool.

But lifestyle was not the only issue addressed in this ad. Security is a primary concern of empty-nesters. Often the active adult homeowner will spend weeks or months away from his or her primary residence traveling, visiting relatives, or wintering in Florida. Living in a community where neighbors look out for each other is another major benefit of Cambridge at Carillon.

Great care needs to be taken when discussing the issues of safety and security. Builders and developers do not want to scare prospective home buyers away nor give the impression that their communities or locations are unsafe. In your ads use phrases such as "peace of mind" or "you'll feel more secure," rather than describe your community as safe or crime-free. In some cases, you would do better not to mention safety or security at all. If it is not uppermost on the minds of your potential buyers, don't put it there.

In the first few weeks this ad appeared, traffic increased by 500 percent. On an average weekend, more than 100 prospective home buyers–all active adults–visited Cambridge at Carillon (Figure 5-2).

Figure 5-2. Many active adults made an appointment to visit after seeing this ad. Actual ad size, 13" x 21"

Attract First-Time Buyers in New Ways

"What's it gonna cost me?" is the question on every first-time home buyer's mind. Price and affordability are the key elements in attracting this prospective homebuyer. In fact, builders often run ads targeted to renters in different sections of the newspaper. Many renters are not aware that they can afford to buy a home, and therefore they are not reading the real estate ads.

Price and affordability are relative. A new home priced in the $80s or $90s may sound like a bargain to a seasoned home shopper. But to a "rookie" buyer, it sounds like a lot of money. The key to communicating affordability is to state the price in terms a first-time buyer can understand. Most first-time buyers are renters. Rent is paid monthly. By translating the total sales price into monthly payments, the first-time buyer can see just how affordable a new home can be.

Washington Homes, Inc., one of the largest home builders in the Greater Washington (D.C.) Metropolitan area, builds condominium homes, townhomes, and single-family homes primary for first-time and first-time move-up buyers. Geaton DeCesaris, Jr., president and CEO of Washington Homes, and his hand-picked marketing team, pride themselves on developing and implementing innovative marketing programs specifically targeted to these buyers.

For example, for customers who lack the immediate resources to make a downpayment on a home, Washington Homes can set up special savings programs. And through its wholly owned mortgage subsidiary, Washington Homes offers a variety of financing packages with monthly payments at manageable levels for many first-time buyers.

Washington Homes also works with one of the largest managers of rental units in the Washington area to offer renters an opportunity to credit a portion of their monthly rent toward the purchase of a home built by Washington Homes. Based on 25 percent accrued credit from a yearly lease, Washington Homes gives residents total credits and incentives of up to 3 percent of the purchase price of a new Washington Home. Many builders have grasped the wisdom of including monthly payments in their ads directed to first-time buyers. Some builders focus on low downpayments, others highlight attractive financing,

Washington Homes chose a more nontraditional route. A series of ads featured the minimum annual salary needed to qualify as a Washington Homes buyer. Single women were shown in the ad primarily because they represented a large percentage of the company's condominium and townhome buyers.

While a disclaimer was included in the ad that "some restrictions apply" and the offer was "subject to approvals," a monthly payment disclaimer was also included in accordance with Regulation Z, Truth in Lending. This regulation, issued by the Board of Governors of the Federal Reserve System, implements the federal Truth in Lending and Fair Credit Billing Acts. Its purpose is to promote informed use of consumer credit by requiring disclosures about its terms and cost.

The headline of the ad, "I make $26,400 a year, and I just bought a Washington Home," is an eye-opener for most first-time buyers. The subhead, "We will make you a homeowner, too." further confirms how easy and affordable owning a Washington Home can be.

This full-page tabloid ad appeared in the *Washington Times* and the *Journal Home Report*. Only those communities with low-end prices were featured in the listings. Significant increases in traffic and sales were reported each time these ads appeared (Figure 5-3).

Figures 5-3. This ad was well targeted. Actual ad size, 10.25" x 12.5".

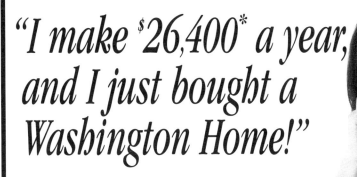

"I make $26,400* a year, and I just bought a Washington Home!"

GRAND OPENING DESIGN SHOWCASE! INTERIOR DECORATOR ON SITE!

We will make you a homeowner, too.

- The most affordable prices
- Great financing – guaranteed interest rate
- First Time Homebuyer's Seminar – call for details

- Special Savings Plans make it easier to own!
- Exciting new designs
- Top quality name brands

To see if you qualify, call 1-800-DIAL-WHI.

TOWNHOMES • From $567 / month°

STAFFORD COUNTY:
- **Potomac Hills - New Section Selling!** - Townhomes from the mid $90's in Quantico. Dir.: Take I-95 S. to Exit 148. Left at stop sign. Go 1/8 mile to right on Rt. 1 S. Go 2 1/2 mi. to Community on right. **(540) 720-5840** or **(703) 690-6014** metro.
- **Hampton Oaks** - 3-Level Townhomes from the low $100's in North Stafford. Dir.: Take I-95 S. to Garrisonville Rd. exit (Exit 143-B). At first light, take left onto Mine Road 1/2 mile to Community on left. **(540) 659-2645** or **(703) 690-0916** metro.

- **Townes at Park Ridge** - 22' wide, 3-Level Garage Townhomes from the $110's in Stafford. Dir.: Take I-95 S. to Garrisonville Road exit (Exit 143-B). Take 610 W. 3 mi. to left on Parkway Boulevard. Sales Center 1/2 mi. on left. **(540) 659-2820** or **(703) 690-4510** metro.
- **Crescents of Park Ridge - Now Selling – Pre-construction Prices!** Luxury 24' wide garage townhomes from the upper $130's. For information call **(540) 659-2820** or **(703) 690-4510** metro.

LOUDOUN COUNTY:
- **Kincaid Forest - New Section Now Selling!** -3-Level Garage Townhomes from the $120's in Leesburg. Dir.: From I-495, take Rt. 7 W. to Rt. 15 S. Turn left at first light onto Sycolin Rd. (Rt.643). Take first left, proceed 1/2 mile to Sales Center on left. **(703) 581-1207.**

PRINCE WILLIAM COUNTY:
- **Townes of Forest Park - Model Grand Opening!** - Luxury 3 & 4-Level Garage 22'-wide Townhomes from the mid $120's in the Montclair area. Dir.: Take I-95 S. to Rt. 234 N. (Exit 152) 1/2 mi. to left on Van Buren St. Make right on Acadia and follow to Models on the right. **(703) 221-5932 or (703) 551-1135** metro.

SINGLE FAMILY HOMES • From $716 / month°

STAFFORD COUNTY:
- **Courts at Park Ridge** - Single family homes from the low $130's in North Stafford. Dir.: Take I-95 S. to Garrisonville Road exit (Exit 143-B). Take 610 W. 3 mi. to left on Parkway Blvd. Sales Center on right. **(504) 659-1880 or (703) 690-2831** metro.

Sales Centers open 11-7 weekdays; 10-6 weekends.
Prices are subject to change without notice. Brokers welcome.

NOW YOU CAN RENT TO OWN A WASHINGTON HOME!
Based on 25% accrued credit from a yearly Equity lease, we'll give Equity residents total credits and incentives of up to 3% of the purchase price of a new Washington Home!

 **Washington Homes®**
Making the American dream affordable®

* 5% 1 year ARM FHA financing, 1 and 5 caps APR 5.793 based on financial examples. Townhome sale price of $95,990 and $93,100 mortgage amount with a payment of $567 per month plus MIP, taxes and insurance. Single family home price of $133,990 and $129,950 mortgage amount with a payment of $716 per month plus MIP, taxes and insurance. All financing available. Some restrictions apply. Rate, terms and program subject to change without notice. Subject to approvals. See Sales Representative for details.

"We are pledged to the letter and spirit of U.S. policy for the achievement of Equal Housing Opportunity throughout the Nation. We encourage and support an affirmative advertising and marketing program in which there are no barriers to obtaining housing because of race, color, religion, sex, handicap, familial status, or national origin."

 WHI Listed NYSE

Whet the Customer's Appetite with a Teaser Ad

Retailers have known for years that by giving the consumer just a taste of what's to come, they usually will be back for more.

Builders can learn from that. Traditionally builders wait until the sales trailer, model, or information center is up and running before they advertise, or until their printed materials are ready to be distributed. But in most cases, you benefit if you advertise your homes or communities as soon as possible.

Prior to an opening, a teaser ad often works successfully. The purpose of this type of ad is to provide just enough information to entice a prospective home buyer to take some form of action. The ad should ask readers to call or visit or simply tell them to look for more information coming soon.

The goal of a teaser ad is to arouse the curiosity or interest of a potential buyer without satisfying it completely. It should not be a smaller, more condensed version of the preview ad.

Westminster Homes, located in North Carolina, wanted to create a teaser ad for one of its new communities. Ellington, in Clayton, a suburb of Raleigh, features affordable single family homes starting in the $110's.

K. M. (Tommy) Thompson, assistant vice president and director of sales and marketing, asked that two copy points be stressed: first, that Ellington is in Johnston County; second, that Westminster Homes, a nationally known homebuilder with an excellent reputation, was now building in this county.

Neither the sales center nor the model was built. A potential buyer could literally see nothing at the site other than dirt. But other builders in the area were advertising, and Westminster Homes wanted to establish itself as a player in the market.

The message to be delivered was simple: "Westminster will soon be building homes in a new community in Johnston County." The graphics were kept to a minimum, and an elevation was the only illustration.

With a straightforward headline, a few lines of copy, a logo, and an elevation, this ad could have looked just like almost every other real estate ad in the newspaper. But by doing something that some builders might consider sacrilege, an ordinary ad became an extraordinary one.

The elevation was rotated 90 degrees to appear sideways in the ad. The headline, "Soon all heads will be turning in Johnston County!" refers not only to the soon-to-open community, but also to the ad which must be turned in order to view the elevation.

This ad attracted the attention not only of large numbers of potential home buyers, but of other builders, industry personnel, and media people as well (Figure 5-4).

Figure 5-4. This ad attracted a great deal of attention. Actual ad size, 6.5" x 10.5".

Break Rules with a Corporate Ad

Why run a corporate ad? Two key reasons come to mind. First, it makes a statement about a builder's credibility. A corporate ad says to a consumer, "Look at what we build. Look at all the places we're building." A corporate ad is also often more cost-efficient for a builder or developer because it advertises many communities within one ad. Additionally corporate ads are usually larger than individual community ads, so the builder can make more of a "splash" and attract more attention.

A builder can highlight a variety of homes, prices and locations. Copy can focus on a builder's awards, reputation, or philosophy. While individual community ads usually convey tangible information (such as number of bedrooms, proximity to schools and shopping, and the like), a corporate ad often focuses more on intangible items (such as feelings, values, and concerns.) It can address issues that home buyers are concerned about. It can also generate excitement by featuring incentives, promotions, or sales.

Kettler Forlines Homes, based in Gaithersburg, Maryland, builds homes primarily for move-up buyers in Maryland and Virginia. Under the direction of Bob Simmons, senior vice president, the company has won numerous awards for its imaginative designs, innovative floorplans, and creative attention to detail. Kettler Forlines Homes is selling in 10 communities with homes starting from the mid $100's to the mid $300's.

Kettler Forlines' homes look different, and "live" differently. And most of the home buyers in the area recognize and appreciate that. But Kettler Forlines' current corporate ad did little to convey the excitement and liveability of their homes or communities

To communicate the uniqueness of Kettler Forlines, a new corporate concept was developed. The underlying theme of the words and graphics was "details make the difference."

The graphics were a surrealistic blending of some of the details found in a typical Kettler Forlines homes, along with a photograph of a home, and one of a family. (And, in compliance with Fair Housing Requirements, a photograph of a minority family was rotated in the ad on a regular basis.)

The ad included a decorative light fixture, a designer faucet, and colorful swatches of fabric, wallpaper, and carpet to whet the appetite of a potential home buyer. The family was dressed casually, à la Eddie Bauer, to convey a down-to-earth, realistic portrait of the people found in a Kettler Forlines neighborhood.

In keeping with the untraditional layout of the ad, copy was kept to a minimum with no headline. Short descriptive phrases were used to communicate the uniqueness of Kettler Forlines Homes.

Listings were grouped by location and keyed to a map. The ad included the equal housing statement rather than the logo to avoid adding another graphic element (Figure 5-5).

Kettler Forlines resisted the urge to fill virtually every inch of space within an ad with information. In fact, the white space in this ad is one of its most important graphic elements–proof positive that what you leave out of an ad is as meaningful as what you put into it.

Figure 5-5. A variety of photographs and an abundance of white space make this ad stand out. Actual ad size, 8.5" x 10"

A SPLASH OF IMAGINATION.

A HEALTHY HELPING OF QUALITY

CRAFTSMANSHIP. LOCATIONS SELECTED ONE-BY-ONE.

HOMES THAT CAN BE PERSONALIZED TO PERFECTION.

KETTLER FORLINES WANTS TO WELCOME YOU HOME.

IN MARYLAND

1. **SENECA - HURRY! ONLY TWO CHOICE HOMES REMAIN! Single family manor homes on 1 plus acre homesites in Laytonsville from the $290's.** Take Beltway to I-270 to Shady Grove Rd. East (Exit #9). Follow Shady Grove Rd. through Muncaster Mill Rd. intersection (becomes Air Park Blvd.) to Rt. 124. Turn right on Rt. 124 and follow to a right onto Warfield Rd. Turn right onto Dorsey Rd. (at Laytonsville Golf Club) and follow to a left onto Rt. 108 to community on left. **(301) 353-1446.**

2. **THE VILLAGES AT SPRING RIDGE - MODEL HOME GRAND OPENING! Frederick's fabulous new singles priced from the mid $100's.** Take I-270 N. approx. 8.5 mi. beyond Montgomery County line to exit for Rt. 85 N./Market St. to Frederick. Go N. on Rt. 85 approx. 1 1/4 mi. to left on I-70 E. Go to Patrick St./Rt. 144 Exit. Turn left on Rt. 144 and go 1.6 mi. to main entrance on left. Follow Spring Ridge Pkwy. to a right on Claridge Dr. S. to right on Fleetwood Ct. to model on left. **(301) 831-4271.**

3. **SPRING RIDGE MANOR HOMES - BEAUTIFULLY DECORATED MODEL! 4-5 bedroom single family homes from the low $200's.** Take I-270 N. approx. 8.5 mi. beyond Montgomery County line to exit for Rt. 85 N./Market St. to Frederick. Go N. on Rt. 85 approx. 1 1/4 mi. to left on I-70 E. Go to Patrick St./Rt. 144 Exit. Turn left on Rt. 144 and go 1.6 mi. to main entrance on left. Go straight ahead to a left on Remington Drive to model on corner of Remington Place. **(301) 831-4243.**

4. **WEST WINDS - Manor Homes in a golf course community from the low $200's.** Take I-270 N. approx. 8.5 mi. past Montgomery County line to exit for Rt. 85 N. (Market St.). Go N. on Rt. 85 approx. 1 1/4 mi. to left on I-70 E. Go to Exit for Rt. 75 N. Follow Rt. 75 N. approx. 2 1/2 mi. to the second Old New London Rd. Turn left and follow to a right on Gas House Pike to a left into West Winds to the Visitors Center on the left. **(301) 831-3821.**

5. **THE VILLAS AT WEST WINDS** - Preview Sales from the $160's. **(301) 831-3821.**

6. **BRANCH HILL - Luxury single family homes on 2 + acres in a quiet setting in Clarksburg from the $330's.** Take Beltway to I-270 to Rt. 121 Boyds/ Clarksburg exit. Go north on Rt. 121 to a left on Rt. 355 to a left on Comus Rd. to first left on Shiloh Church Rd. to community on right. **(301) 353-1446.**

IN VIRGINIA

7. **LAKEPOINTE AT ASHBURN VILLAGE – From the mid $200's.** Take Beltway to Rt. 7 W. Go approx. 2 mi. past Rt. 28 to left at Ashburn Village entrance... or ... take Beltway to Dulles Toll Road to Exit for Rt. 28 N. Follow approx. 1 1/2 mi. to a left on Rt. 625 (Waxpool Rd.) which changes to Rt. 640. Follow to Ashburn Village Blvd. to a left onto Cheltenham (1st left). Follow Cheltenham into LakePointe to Sales Center on left. **(703) 589-1003.**

8. **ALEXANDRA'S GROVE AT BELMONT - AWARD WINNING COMMUNITY! Single family homes from the mid $200's.** Take Beltway to Rt. 7 W. Go approx. 3 mi. past Rt. 28 to a left onto Rt. 659. Belmont Ridge Rd. Follow Belmont Ridge Rd. to a left onto Stubble Rd. Follow Stubble Rd. through entry on right to model on left. **(703) 581-1209.**

9. **WILLOW OAK - HURRY ONLY 2 HOMES REMAIN! Luxurious single family homes in Alexandria from the mid $300's.** Take Beltway to Exit # 2 S., Telegraph Rd. Follow Telegraph Rd. approx. 3 mi. to community on left and Sales Center on right. **(301) 353-1446.**

10. **HUNTERS RIDGE - FURNISHED MODEL GRAND OPENING! New single family homes from the mid $200's!** Take Beltway to I-95 S. to Prince William Pkwy. exit (W.). Follow Pkwy. approx. 4 mi. to traffic signal where Pkwy. turns left. Turn left and follow approx. 3 mi. to community on left. **(703) 791-4508.**

11. **RIVERSCAPE** - Luxury Homes in Great Falls. Call **(301) 353-1446** for more information.

For more information on any of our fine communities or sales center hours please call (301) 258-0980 or any of our individual communities.

"We are pledged to the letter and spirit of U.S. policy for the achievement of Equal Housing Opportunity throughout the nation. We encourage and support an affirmative advertising and marketing program in which there are no barriers to obtaining housing because of race, color, religion, sex, handicap, familial status, or national origin."

Prices subject to change without notice. Brokers Welcome. Member Suburban MD and Northern VA Building Industry Associations.

KETTLER • FORLINES • HOMES

Talk About a Great Idea: Testimonial Advertising

Consumers have become conditioned to expect companies to brag about their products. However most consumers take such comments lightly.

But throw in a testimonial by product, and the credibility of that product increases greatly. Consider the success of the television infomercial. This carefully staged, long-format commercial is often designed to look like a television talk or news magazine show. While the host or hostess leads the discussion, testimonials from people in the audience or from people who have been videotaped earlier constitute the bulk of the show.

Home shopping networks also use testimonials to help sell their merchandise. While a certain item is shown on the screen, viewers are invited to call in and praise the product.

Builders and developers should take note. Testimonials can be a highly effective way of reaching the target market. But just as you can find more than one way to feature a home in an ad, you can find more than one way to feature a testimonial in an ad.

Fox Ridge Homes, based in Nashville, has been building homes in middle Tennessee since 1960. Under the leadership of Al Davis, CEO, Fox Ridge Homes' reputation for quality, value, and customer satisfaction has grown significantly. In fact, many Fox Ridge homeowners are repeat buyers. And many sales are attributed to word-of-mouth referrals from current homeowners.

Fox Ridge wanted to share its homeowner's positive and enthusiastic comments with potential home buyers, but it did not want a traditional testimonial ad. Typical testimonial ads featured photographs, often of models posing as home buyers, along with a quote. Fox Ridge Homes wanted to feature several quotes from several different homeowners.

Two concepts were created–and both eventually used. The first ad, headlined, "Words to live by" featured a large elevation with seven quotes designed as callouts from the home. The quotes addressed such issues as design, quality, service, location, floor plans, neighborhood, and financing.

None of the quotes were attributed to any particular person. But the subhead, "Our homeowners know us best" implies that these quotes are indeed from Fox Ridge homeowners (Figure 5-6A).

The second ad, with the headline, "A few words from our family of 7,000 homeowners" featured one-word quotes from actual homeowners. Elevations were shown from the communities in which these people lived. Because the quotes were shorter than in the other testimonial ad, the body copy was longer and more detailed (Figure 5-6B).

These ads were well received by potential home buyers, as well as by Fox Ridge Home's sales staff as well. Because of this success, Fox Ridge Homes developed a series of oversized postcards based on the testimonial concept. One set of postcards featured homeowner testimonials; another set featured testimonials from the broker community. Fox Ridge Homes campaign increased traffic by over 40 percent.

Figures 5-6. Testimonial ads need not include photographs of the people quoted. Actual ad sizes, 8.5" x 11".

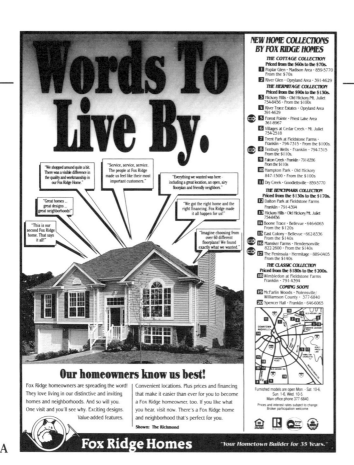

Send Season's Greetings
Every Season of the Year

Major corporations conduct extensive research and spend huge sums of money in developing their product's logo, packaging, and advertising. With so much time, effort, and money invested, these companies understandably are reluctant to make changes over time–especially if they are still well received.

But with so many new products and services being introduced into the marketplace each year, a company must constantly freshen up its product's image to keep it foremost in the mind of the consumer. These advertisers don't want a potential buyer to look at their ads and think "it's the same old thing."

Even a successful ad can become stagnant over time. When that happens, many advertisers substitute an ad that's part of the same campaign. By using a variation on the same theme, a new ad can often capitalize on the success of its predecessor. Consider the excellent example set by the Milk Marketing Board, whose ads feature famous people wearing milk mustaches.

The Cavalcade of Homes in Naperville, Illinois, was taking place directly across the street from High Meadow, a community of affordable custom homes. In order to attract the attention of visitors to the Cavalcade, and urge them to stop by High Meadow while they were in the area, a one-time-only ad was developed for the Cavalcade magazine.

A photo of a young boy in an oversized baseball cap trying to look up was the only graphic in the ad headlined, "Heads Up!" The body copy–which was purposely kept to a minimum–alerted Cavalcade visitors to the fact that High Meadow was just across the street (Figure 5-7A).

Everyone liked this ad–from potential home buyers to salespeople and brokers. Because it was so well received, the original ad was revised to run in the *Chicago Tribune* and other local publications. But as the warmth of summer faded and autumn approached, the appropriateness of the ad featuring a boy in shorts and a short-sleeved shirt came into question.

Rather than go back to the drawing board to develop a totally different ad, the agency suggested the ad become part of a campaign featuring two boys (one Caucasian and one Afro-American) in different seasonal sports gear. Because both boys appeared in every ad, Fair Housing Requirements were met.

The fall ad showed the boys in soccer uniforms with a headline that read, "What a kick!" (Figure 5-7B). The body copy remained the same. Only the subhead was changed.

An ad featuring basketball included the headline, "Great Move!" (Figure 5-7C).While the football ad asked potential home buyers, "In the game for a great new home? Look no further."(Figure 5-7D).

Macom Corporation and Moser Enterprises, which jointly developed High Meadow, were delighted with the positive response to this ad campaign. Traffic increased 10 percent during the time that these ads ran in the newspapers. Many prospects brought the ads with them to the sales office.

Figures 5-7. This well-targeted campaign helped High Meadow increase traffic and sales. Actual ad sizes, 6.5" x 10.5".

A

B

C

D

Market a Community as a Destination

Pick up any travel brochure and be swept away by beautiful photographs and poetic words that paint an inviting picture of fantasy islands and exotic destinations. These brochures go far beyond just whetting the appetite of a would-be traveler. Because so many resorts, cruise lines, and vacation spots are competing for the same vacation dollars, travel industry professionals know that their advertising and marketing materials must entice and excite potential visitors. In effect, they must make consumers "fall in love" with the idea of visiting their resorts.

Builders and developers of planned developments or resort communities should take a page from the travel industry's book on advertising. These communities should be positioned as "destinations," or exciting places that are worth seeing, rather than as just neighborhoods. By positioning a community as a destination, rather than just a collection of homes, potential home buyers have added incentive to visit and buy.

Snyder Hunt Realty is the developer of Wyndham, the premier master planned community in Richmond, Virginia. This beautiful community has 30 distinctive neighborhoods, the private Dominion Golf and Country Club featuring a par-72 golf course designed by Curtis Strange and a magnificent 28,000 square foot clubhouse, a separate community swim and tennis club, walking paths, nature trails, a 22-acre lake, on-site offices, shopping, and a new elementary school.

More than 700 families already call this award-winning community home. Though it has positioned itself as the area's premier master planned community, it is not the only master planned community in Richmond. Competition has steadily increased. But, while other communities have amenities, Wyndham is in a class by itself.

A review of the real estate section in the *Richmond Times Dispatch* revealed several competitors of Wyndham were running larger ads. Though these communities were not as impressive as Wyndham in size or scope, they gave the perception of having more to offer.

The marketing team for Wyndham determined that the community needed to reestablish itself as the best in the area. The first step was to substantially increase the size of the ads. To further emphasize the Wyndham difference and attract the attention of home buyers, a four-color ad was used for the first insertion.

Jerry Van Houten, vice president of sales and marketing for Wyndham, provided the direction for the new ads: "Wyndham is more than just homes; it's a better way of life." In order to stress the community name, the word, "*Wyndham*" was used as the headline. The subhead summed it all up: "The Homes. The Life. The Style."

Body copy focused on the unique style of living available only at Wyndham and highlighted the many of on-site amenities. The primary graphic was a panoramic photograph of the gazebo, lake, and Dominion Club. The ad also included a photograph of one of the homes and a lifestyle photograph. The widely varying price range of available homes at Wyndham appears under the elevation, directly above the gazebo in the center of the ad. In this position, the prices are easy to spot (Figure 5-8).

Research should drive the advertising effort. Snyder Hunt conducted extensive research and determined that potential home buyers wanted to see photographs or renderings of the homes. Buyers also were unaware of the wide price range of homes available at Wyndham. Many assumed they could not afford to purchase there.

The newly designed ads were based on this research. A complete listing of Wyndham neighborhoods and price ranges, grouped in ascending order, was placed beneath the clubhouse photograph. This listing allowed potential home buyers to see that Wyndham literally had "something for everyone."

Traffic to this elegant and distinctive community increased dramatically. And, just as important, Wyndham's ads accurately reflected the superior quality of the homes, the lifestyle, and the setting to be found there.

Figure 5-8. This ad was the picture of elegance for this golf course community. Actual ad size, 10" x 13"

WYNDHAM

The Homes. The Life. The Style.

Here, in the area's premier master planned community you'll enjoy a world of luxury, comfort, fun and peace-of-mind. Our homeowners enjoy a year-round lifestyle that includes the Wyndham Swim & Racquet Club, planned events and activities and miles of walking and nature trails. And, of course, there's The Dominion Club and golf course providing a breathtaking backdrop to all we have to offer. Come stroll our quiet cul-de-sac streets and meet our friendly neighbors. You'll feel safe, secure, at home. Wyndham. It's where you want to live.

Enjoy tennis at the Wyndham Swim and Racquet Club.

Call 804-360-1100 for details.

The Barrington
By Eagle Construction Co. of Virginia, Inc.

The Sycamore
By Parker Lancaster, Inc.

The Peachtree
By J.R. Walker Company, Inc.

The Maymont
By Mike Dumont Construction Co., Inc.

The Baird
By Boone, Boone, Loeb & Pettit, Inc.

SINGLE FAMILY HOMES

- **Aubury** - From the $120's to $150's
- **Maybrook** - From the $140's to $185,000
- **Collinstone** - From the $150's to $190's
- **Glencrest** - From the $190's to $240's
- **Chestnut Hill** - From the $210's to $250's
- **Glen Abbey** - From the $220's to $280's
- **Benning Oaks** - From the $240's to $290's
- **Brentmoor** - From the $240's to $350,000
- **Hardwick** - From the $260's to $325,000
- **Manor Park** - From the $270's to $315,000
- **Chadsworth Landing** - From the $270's to $400's
- **Ascot Glen** - From the $280's to $360's
- **Stoneacre** - From the $300's to $450,000
- **Treyburn** - From the $320's to $455,000
- **Cherry Hill II** - Custom homes from the $360's to $700's

TOWNHOMES, COURTYARD HOMES & VILLAS

- **Morgan's Glen** - Townhomes from the $150's to $270's
- **Kelston Green** - Maintenance-free Courtyard homes from the $180's to $220's
- **The Fairways** - Golf Villas from the $220's to $280's

Directions: Take I-64 West to I-295 to the Nuckols Rd. North exit. Wyndham is two miles ahead on the right. HTTP://:WWW.BNT.COM/~SNYDERH/WYNDHAM

Another Distinctive **SNYDER HUNT** *Community*

Communicate Several Messages in One Ad

The facts are mind-boggling. Billions of dollars are spent annually on advertising. The average American is bombarded by over 300,000 advertising messages a year. And that number is conservative. People are receiving an average of 820 messages per person, per day. Of that daily number, a person will notice fewer than 90 of those messages, and remember only 15 for a 24-hour period.

The bottom line? Wherever a builder or developer advertises–in newspaper, magazine, radio, television, or internet–the sales message must stand out from the competition. One way to make an ad noticeable is to simplify what the ad says and how the ad looks. Too many messages or too many similar-sized graphics force the consumer to work too hard to read and understand the ad. The more an advertiser puts in an ad, the easier it is for that ad to be overlooked.

Many of the most effective ads focus on communicating one key feature or benefit. Consider Maytag appliances and its never-busy repairman. Maytag's reliability has been successfully stressed in print and broadcast ads for years.

But what if a builder has several equally important messages to convey to potential home buyers? Can such an ad stand out in the crowd and attract the attention of its target market? The answer is a resounding "Yes!" if the headline is strong and the graphics are eye-catching. The successful ad for Millpointe West is a perfect example.

Crosswinds Communities, the second largest homebuilder in Detroit, Michigan, has won many awards for its innovatively designed, affordably priced homes. One of the first single-family home communities they developed was Millpointe in the Detroit suburbs. The homes, priced from $75,990, featured vaulted ceilings, gourmet kitchens, and attached two-car garages. The community sold out in record time.

Drawing on the success of the Millpointe name, Bernie Glieberman, president of Crosswinds, developed several other similarly named communities. Among them was Millpointe West in the Ann Arbor-Ypsilanti area. The ad, targeted to first-time buyers, had three key points to get across. Each point addressed a concern of their target market.

Instead of featuring these points in the headline, the ad's headline directly addressed the target market. "New Home Buyers, Take Note!" is a double-entendre that refers to both the ad in general, and the "notes" within the ad.

Each of the three key points was featured on its own graphic element. The low downpayment appeared on a note with a push pin in it. The affordable price was on a taped note, while the excellent schools appeared on a page that was ripped out of a memo pad.

The primary graphic of the ad was a large elevation that showed prospective buyers how much home they were getting for such an affordable price. This information-packed ad attracted so many prospects that the advertising had to be canceled after only a few months (Figure 5-9).

Figure 5-9. An ad worth noting–by home buyers and home builders alike. Actual ad size, 6.5" x 10".

Give Home Buyers the Inside Story

Car manufacturers understand well the concept that every story has two sides. Their advertising materials show both the outside and the inside of their automobiles. After all, no matter how nice the outside looks, the inside of the car is where buyers will be spending most of their time.

If you look through any new car brochure, you will notice how much of the information focuses on the inside details of the automobile. Photographs and copy focus on how comfortable, convenient, and luxurious the car's interior is. Advertising copy highlights the "driveability" of the car–in other words, the pleasure derived from owning and driving that car.

The ultimate goal of these advertising materials is to make the buyer fall in love with that new car, which, coincidentally, is the same response that home builders should aim for when they advertise their homes.

A recent focus group on home buyer's advertising preferences, held by a builder in Washington, DC, revealed that seeing the inside of the home was often more important than seeing the outside of it. After all, just as new car buyers would be spending the bulk of their time inside the car, the new home buyers would be spending most of their time inside the house.

Potential home buyers participating in the focus study wanted to see what the kitchen, living room, and family room looked like. They wanted to be able to picture how they would live their lives in that new home. These buyers were more concerned with the functionality and liveability of that home, not just its curb appeal.

Toll Brothers, Inc., based in Huntington Valley, a suburb of Philadelphia, is the largest luxury home builder in the United States. The company has communities in 13 states and is listed on the New York Stock Exchange. Among the firm's many awards are America's Best Builder, National Builder of the Year and the National Housing Quality Award.

Traditionally Toll Brothers' ads feature exterior photographs. And, while these ads have been quite successful, Zvi Barzilay, executive vice president, wanted to showcase the exciting interiors of the homes, as well.

A series of full-page ads each featured one dramatic interior photograph. The first ad highlighted the spectacular two-story family room with its soaring ceiling and wall of oversized windows. The headline addressed the dazzling amount of height and space: "Ceilings that take you to new heights ." Copy, kept to a minimum, described the innovative details to be found within a Toll Brothers home.

Note the Andersen™ window logo in the bottom of the ad. Andersen™ is one of many national manufacturers and suppliers that participate in coop advertising programs. While guidelines vary according to each manufacturer, these companies agree to pay a portion of the ad cost in return for the display of their logo and/or mention of their product.

Cooperative advertising makes sense–especially when the product has a nationwide reputation for quality. And so does giving a prospective home buyer a glimpse into what lies beyond the front door of a home. The more easily a buyer falls in love with a home, the more easily you can convince the prospect to buy it.

Just ask Toll Brothers, the company experienced a 100 percent increase in deposits, when more than 3,100 prospective buyers visited their communities after this ad appeared (Figure 5-10).

Figure 5-10. Show off your home's exciting or innovative features. Actual ad size, 13" x 21".

Reach the Parents Via the Children

A few years back, Pepsi Cola ran a television commercial that featured a tiny, curly-headed tot giggling hysterically as a litter of puppies playfully jumped all over him. Was Pepsi trying to sell their cola to toddlers? Of course, not. The people at Pepsi, and their highly paid market research company, knew that the irresistibility of the little boy and his dogs would reflect favorably upon their soft drink. No parent (or dog lover) could watch that commercial without a smile. In effect, Pepsi was betting that the good feelings created by the TV spot would positively effect the buying habits of its target market.

Similarly Walt Disney World frequently runs TV commercials featuring children scampering through the Magic Kingdom as their dreams come true. What parent would not want the same for his or her child?

These commercials and dozens like them use the emotional appeal of a child to tug at the heart strings of the adult. Builders should know that the saying, "Nothing steals the show like a dog or kid," is true. When your target market is young families, showing children in your ads provides a great way to get ahead of your competition, too.

Duffy Homes, one of the largest and most successful home builders in Columbus, Ohio, builds primarily for move-up buyers. The majority of these buyers are families with children. Regis Skeehan, vice president of operations at Duffy Homes, wanted the corporate ads to directly target this group of potential home buyers.

The move-up home buyer's market in the Columbus area was highly competitive. Duffy Homes positioned itself as offering more freedom of choice, greater flexibility and customization. Because its competitors were more rigid about changes, options and upgrades, this position gave Duffy a definite advantage over them.

While most builders featured only photographs or renderings of their homes, several did show their target market in their ads. But Duffy wanted its advertising to be as graphically different as the company. Rather than feature a square photograph of a family or a few children within the border of its ad, the ad agency literally "popped" a quartet of chil-

dren from the top of the ad. Three of the children hold onto or lean upon what appears to be the border of the ad. But the tops of the children's heads are the actual border of the ad (Figure 5-11).

The headline communicates Duffy's customization policy and ties in nicely to the primary graphic. The map and listings are well organized and easy to read. Note the cooperative logos in the bottom of the ad. Duffy Homes has taken advantage of the supplier's cooperative advertising programs. The high quality of the suppliers says a lot to potential home buyers about the high quality of Duffy homes.

Remember, too, that cooperative advertising is not limited to newspaper or magazine ads. Duffy Homes developed a four-page features insert for its community brochures to prominently mention and display many of their top-quality suppliers.

Did qualified traffic increase when Duffy Homes ran this child's-play ad? Absolutely.

Figure 5-11. Focusing on children attracts the attention of move-up buyers. Actual ad size, 6.5" x 11".

We Make Customizing Your New Home Child's Play!

Now designing your own **Duffy** home is as easy as A-B-C and 1-2-3 with our latest, perhaps greatest advantage ... flexibility! No need to worry about what comes standard or what's an option. With Duffy Homes, just choose the floor plan you like best – then personalize it as much (or as little) as you like. Our experienced sales consultants will help you select options and upgrades that create a dream home uniquely your own! Quite simply, Duffy Homes offers you more choice, flexibility, and advantages than any other builder. Visit one of our fine communities today.

MODEL LOCATIONS

❶ Academy Ridge - Gahanna:
I-270 to Morse Rd. exit; east on Morse Rd. to Hamiliton Rd.; right (south) on Hamilton Rd. to the community entrance on your right. **From the $200's 471-8050**

❷ Bristol Commons - Dublin: I-270 to the Dublin exit; west on Rte. 161 to Avery Rd.; right (north) on Avery Rd. to Brand Rd.; right (east) on Brand Rd. to Bristol Commons on your left. **From the $240's 889-0200**

❸ Carrington Place - Hilliard: I-270 to Tuttle Crossing exit; west on Tuttle Crossing to Wilcox Rd.; left (south) on Wilcox Rd. to Hayden Run Rd.; left (east) on Hayden Run Rd. to Britton; right (south) on Britton to Carrington Place on your right. **From the low $200's 876-2967**

❹ Falcon Ridge - Powell: I-270 to Rte. 315 north to Powell Rd.; left (west) on Powell Rd. to Bennett Pkwy.; left on Bennett Pkwy. into the subdivision. **From the $220's 844-5024**

❺ Glenshire - Pickerington: I-270 to I-70 east; take Rte. 256 South/ Pickerington exit to Rte. 204 & go left (east) on Rte. 204 to Waterton Dr. into the subdivision. **From the $230's 759-0778**

❻ Medallion Estates - Westerville: I-270 to Rte. 161 to the Sunbury Rd. exit; right (north) on Sunbury Rd. for several miles past the intersection of County Line Rd.–to the golf course and Medallion Dr. on your left. **From the $300's 882-5969**

PEACHTREE
Non-stop warranty

CORIAN
DUPONT

COMFORT ASSURED
Electric heat pumps heat, cool and save.

FRIGIDAIRE
BUILT FOR GENERATIONS

Duffy Homes
An Edwards Company

EQUAL HOUSING OPPORTUNITY

Model Home Hours:
Mon.-Thurs. 1-7, Fri. Closed, Sat. 12-5, Sun. 12-6.

BIA
REGISTERED BUILDER

To Reach New Target Markets
Redefine a Builder's Image

Wayne Homes builds customized homes at affordable prices on the buyer's lots in primarily rural areas of Ohio. In essence, Wayne Homes builds "when you want it, where you want it, and how you want it."

They offer two collections of homes, The Artistry Collection and the Renaissance Collection.

Artistry Collection homes range from 1,040 to 2,280 square feet. with base prices from the $50s. The primary target market for these homes is young families, mostly first-time buyers. Price, size, and value are important to these people. The home is the center of their lives. How the home functions is key. They say, "Show me what I'm getting for my money."

Renaissance Collection homes range from 1,939 to 2,669 square feet with base prices from the $90s. The primary buyers for these homes are slightly older, better educated, and earn more than buyers for Artistry Collection homes. These prospects are often move-up buyers who do not want to compromise. Quality and value are important to these buyers. Their homes are more of a retreat and a place to entertain. What the homes look like is key. Less of their lifestyle revolves around their homes. They say, "Show me how my life will be easier, more comfortable, more enjoyable in this home."

Wayne Homes positions itself as a high-volume builder of affordable customized homes on buyers' lots. Wayne Homes provides many benefits for the consumer. However its advertising did little to communicate these benefits.

Several problems needed to be addressed. Dave Showers, chief executive officer of Wayne Homes and his staff made the job easier by providing excellent market research that gave highly detailed profiles of the company's current buyers. This information focused directly on the primary buyers.

Separate ads were recommended for each collection, because the two groups of target market buyers have different ideas of how a home should look and how it should function. However each ad was designed with a similar border treatment that prominently displayed the Wayne Homes logo. The primary difference was that the collection name was included above the logo.

The Artistry ads were designed to paint a picture of who lives in the home to help the target market see themselves in these homes. The ads emphasized price and highlighted product and maps. Most of these buyers have children and were looking for more room. Therefore the ad featured a photograph of a girl hanging upside down (Figure 5-12A). To comply with the Fair Housing laws, the same ad was prepared with a minority boy in the same position. A detailed rotation schedule was sent with each ad stat (Figure 5-12B).

The Renaissance Collection ads focused on the imaginative designs. Price was still a factor, but it was not of primary importance. To emphasize the new designs, the shape of an actual window from one of the houses formed the border of the ad. The product was shown in a larger size than in the Artistry Collection ads (Figure 5-12C).

Because no other builder featured children in their ads, the Artistry Collection ads graphically stood apart from the rest–even though many of the ads were relatively small in size. The Renaissance Collection ads with their unusual border also attracted a great deal of attention. Name recognition increased, as did calls and visits to the sales centers.

Figures 5-12A and 5-12B. Potential home buyers responded strongly to these well-targeted ads. Figure 5-12C. You can use design features as graphics in your ad. Actual ad sizes, 4" x 5".

A

B

C

CHAPTER SIX

PROBLEMS, SOLUTIONS, RESULTS

Recent winners of National Sales and Marketing Awards are featured on the following pages. Keep in mind, these ads were award winners for more than just their innovative copy or layout design. Each produced measurable results–in the form of increased traffic.

Problem

The developer wanted to increase awareness of this luxury custom home community.

Solution

Testimonial ads were developed featuring actual residents in front of their homes. For added interest the headline type was interspersed with the body copy (Figure 6-1).

Results

One thousand additional people visited the community over a 1-month period.

Development: StoneFields
Developer: Lakeside Development Company
*   Mequon, Wisconsin*

National Sales and Marketing Awards Silver Award Winner

"When we decided to build, about the only things we weren't looking for were surprises. You know,

"Obviously, ADVENTURE is something

you always hear the horror stories. But we went with Lakeside. They really take care of the details.

I LOOK FOR at the *other*

The craftsmanship was phenomenal. We got a lot of home for the money. Besides, how many people

end of my DRIVEWAY."

do you know of who can actually say building a house was a great experience."

Lakeside Development Company ~ 1535 W. Market Street, Mequon, Wisconsin 53092 ~ (414) 241-2300

Figure 6-1. Actual ad size, 8.25" x 11"

Problem

The developer wanted to communicate the fact that a wide variety of golf course homesites and views were available in this master-planned community.

Solution

A graphically appealing color ad was designed featuring the golf course layout (Figure 6-2).

Results

In the 2 years since it opened, an average of 10 homes were sold each month.

Development: Indian Peaks
Developer: McStain Enterprises
            Boulder, Colorado
Creative: Miles Advertising
            Greenwood Village, Colorado

National Sales and Marketing Awards Silver Award Winner

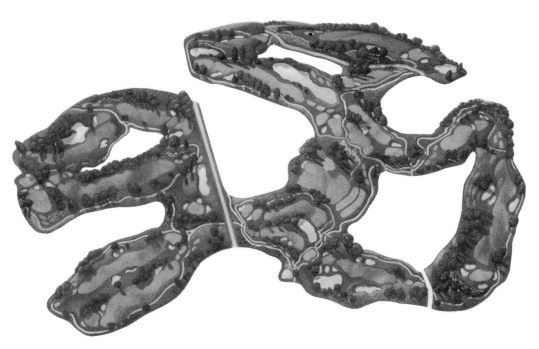

When you buy a home at McStain's Indian Peaks master-planned community, you get to pick out a lot more than just tile, carpeting and paint color. You can also choose whether you'd like to look out your back window at a peaceful fairway, a quiet green, or the winding trials of an open space park.

Because only Indian Peaks offers you four unique neighborhoods tucked away around the beauty of a Hale-Irwin designed golf course. And built around the idea that you and your family deserve quiet, winding streets, plenty of room to experience nature, and a variety of warm, friendly homes.

From our turn-of-the-century Village Green neighborhood and our patio homes at Lilac Hill, to our two exquisite custom home communities, you'll find attention to detail and a commitment to nurturing neighborhoods, and the natural habitat around them.

Winner- 1995 Mame Grand Award for best master-planned community

You'll find wonderful McStain touches like a central park in Village Green to encourage more family picnics. Or the fact that Lilac Hill's luxurious patio homes sit on a hill with terraced streets so each home has a view of the mountains. Or, the unique variety of builders and styles our breathtaking custom homes offer.

It's the best of four worlds. It's the best of all kinds of floorplans. It's the best place to mark an "x," and call it home.

Indian Peaks is located just minutes from Boulder off Baseline and 95th. Village Green offers six plans and starts in the $180s. 665-8200. Lilac Hill has six styles of patio homes starting in the low $200s. 665-1055. Custom homes are available at Starlight Ridge from the mid $200s, call 666-8800 and at Eagle's Wing from the $300s, call 665-1200.

McSTAIN
FEELS LIKE HOME

DRAW AN **X** WHERE YOU'D LIKE YOUR BACKYARD TO BE.

Figure 6-2. Actual ad size, 16.5" x 10.75"

Problem

Every builder in this planned community was offering some form of incentive or discount. The developer wanted to increase traffic to the community.

Solution

A promotional ad was created with a large price tag featuring $0 and the names of participating builders. The free options and a cash discount were listed below (Figure 6-3).

Results

Because none of the options was tied to a specific builder, potential home buyers had to visit each one to determine what was being offered. Traffic increased 35 percent during the 2 weeks of the promotion.

Development: Hunter's Green
Developer: Markborough Florida
        Tampa, Florida
Creative: King/Matson Advertising
        Tampa, Florida

National Sales and Marketing Awards Silver Award Winner

It's Fall.
Look What Fell.
Purchase A Home This Weekend At Hunter's Green And Put This Price Tag On One Of The Options Below.

Fireplace   *Upgraded landscaping*   *Outdoor kitchen*   *Pool*   *Spa*   *Cash discount*

This weekend, Tampa Bay's fastest-selling community will sell even faster. Because the 11 premier home builders at Hunter's Green are giving away valuable options worth thousands. Pools, backyard spas, outdoor kitchens, beautiful fireplaces, upgraded landscaping and more, or even cash discounts—when you purchase a beautiful new home in our private, master-planned community. Several homes are even available for immediate occupancy.

So stop by our Model & Visitor Center today for a map to all our villages and models. Open Monday–Saturday, 10am–6pm; Sunday, Noon–6pm. Broker participation encouraged.

HUNTER'S GREEN

Homes from low $100's to over $1 million.

8709 Hunter's Green Drive • Tampa, Florida 33647 • (813) 973-2000
One mile east of I-75 (Exit 56) on Bruce B. Downs Blvd. (CR 581)

Figure 6-3. Actual ad size, 10.5 x 17.75"

Problem

The builder wanted to communicate multiple reasons for choosing the company's homes.

Solution

This ad, part of a multimedia campaign, featured both the emotional and practical reasons to buy a home (Figure 6-4).

Results

The builder noted an increase in first-quarter sales, and many buyers took advantage of the financing package.

Development: Six communities of Falcon Homes
Builder: Falcon Homes
*   Englewood, Colorado*
Creative: Miles Advertising
*   Greenwood Village, Colorado*

National Sales and Marketing Awards Gold Award Winner

Maybe not as often as you like.

But there are moments

of eating chocolate ice cream without remorse.

And giving yourself the opportunity

to spread out in large, open spaces.

To fill big walk-in closets and

surrender deeply into a Jacuzzi tub.

It isn't a crime, after all,

to have so many blessings.

6.99% *You follow your head*

as well as your heart.

And you look for opportunities where both agree.

6.99% 1st year

7.99% 2nd year

8.99% the balance of the 30 year loan.
9.398% APR based on a 10% down payment.*
Other financing options available.

1. Stonegate
(303) 841-4119
From the
upper $100's

**2. Lone Tree &
Country Club
Estates**
(303) 649-1010
From the
low $300's

3. Wildcat Ridge
(303) 790-1325
From the
low $200's

**4. Manor Knolls
at Highlands
Ranch**
(303) 470-0711
From the
upper $100's

**5. The Greens at
Castle Pines
Village**
(303) 688-0236
From the
low $300's

6. Willow Park
(303) 841-6610
From the
upper $100's

Call our relocation hotline at 1-800-792-5806

*Disclosure: Offer good only while supply of financing lasts. Special financing only available through Falcon Mortgage, L.P. and is for new contracts only. Offer good on limited inventory of Falcon Homes. The maximum loan amount is $203,150. Program applies to 90% loan to value or less.
Home must close on or before April 15, 1995. Falcon Homes reserves the right to change or withdraw this offer at any time without notice.

Figure 6-4. Actual ad size, 13" x 10.5"

Problem

In a market surrounded by large subdivisions, this community provided a smaller alternative.

Solution

A photograph reminiscent of a Norman Rockwell painting graced in an ad depicting Franklin Chase as an intimate neighborhood. (Figure 6-5).

Results

Almost half of the prospective buyers who visited mentioned the ad.

Development: Franklin Chase
Developer: Douglass Properties, Inc.
      Raleigh, North Carolina

National Sales and Marketing Awards Silver Award Winner

Figure 6-5. Actual ad size, 10.5 x 13.25"

Problem

The builder wanted to reach renters and other first-time home buyers who didn't know they could afford to own a home.

Solution

A 2-page ad featured the target market. The nontraditional placement appealed to a first-time buyer (Figure 6-6).

Results

More than 700 prospective buyers visited during the time this ad appeared.

Development: Meadowview
Developer: McStain Enterprises
        Boulder, Colorado
Creative: Miles Advertising
        Greenwood Village, Colorado

National Sales and Marketing Awards Gold Award Winner

Figure 6-6. Actual ad size, 10.25" x 8"

important to first-time home buyers. But affordability is not only feature they look for.

Solution

An eye-catching border treatment of flowers and triangles surrounds this ad. The headline addresses the charm of the community, while the body copy emphasizes the affordability of the homes (Figure 6-7).

Results

This ad brought in 400 qualified home buyers.

Development: Summerfield
Builder: Coscan Davidson Homes
     Del Mar, California
Creative: Franklin Stoorza
     San Diego, California

National Sales and Marketing Awards Silver Award Winner

Figure 6-7. Actual ad size, 9.25" x 11.5"

Problem

The developer wanted to raise awareness of this golf-and-country club community.

Solution

A four-color ad showcased the beautiful natural setting, as well as the golf course amenities of the community (Figure 6-8).

Results

During the 5 months that the ad ran, almost 300 prospective home buyers visited, and sales averaged 11.5 a month.

Development: Lowes Island at Cascades
Developer: Bondy Way Development Corporation
      Chevy Chase, Maryland
Creative: Siddall, Matus & Coughter
      Richmond, Virginia

National Sales and Marketing Awards Silver Award Winner

Were the Potomac not right here, it would still be the premier golf and country club community in Northern Virginia.

But the river is here. And with it, an equally spectacular selection of homes, condominiums and town-homes, including town-homes fronting the golf course. One and two-acre estate lots will be available soon.

Become a Lowes Island resident, and you'll be entitled to all the pleasures of Cascades: the pool and tennis courts of the Cascades Community Center, the public links and boat launches of Algonkian Regional Park. And starting this summer, more swimming and tennis

A RIVER ALMOST RUNS THROUGH IT.

at the Lowes Island Recreation Center.

But what you'll really enjoy is living beside two 18-hole golf courses, eight tennis courts, the shimmering

pool and the handsome clubhouse of the private Lowes Island Club. The first championship course, designed by Tom Fazio, is now open along the river.

And so is your invitation to join us. From the Beltway, go 10 miles west on Route 7, turn right onto Algonkian Parkway (Holly Knoll Drive), go 2.5 miles, turn right

onto Lowes Island Boulevard, and look for the Visitor Center on the left. For more information call (703) 450-0808.

LOWES ISLAND AT CASCADES
COUNTRY CLUB AND RESIDENCES

Figure 6-8. Actual ad size, 14.25" x 12.5"

Problem

In a highly competitive, luxury home market, this community needed to attract attention.

Solution

This oversized ad featured watercolor illustrations that conveyed the upscale nature of the homes and community. The headline focused on the limited opportunity to own a home at Longboat Key (Figure 6-9).

Results

More than 100 qualified prospective home buyers visited as a result of this ad.

Development: Vizcaya at Longboat Key
Builder: The EcoGroup, Inc.
Longboat Key, Florida
Creative: United Landmark Associates, Inc.
Tampa, Florida

National Sales and Marketing Awards Silver Award Winner

Figure 6-9. Actual ad size, 21.25" x 11.75"

Problem

Area schools were a major concern of the families considering
a move into this community.

Solution

Because neighboring districts had eliminated all creative arts courses,
while the school district serving Fisher's Landing had not, a 2-page
full-color ad featured a group of school children playing the violin
(Figure 6-10).

Results

Sales held steady at 25 per month, nearly triple the amount of
the competition.

Development: Fisher's Landing
Developer: Newland Northwest
*   Camas, Washington*
Creative: Inter Communications Inc.
*   Newport Beach, California*
National Sales and Marketing Awards Silver Award Winner

Figure 6-10. Actual ad size, 28.75" x 11"

agate line–A unit of measurement for advertising space, one column wide and 1/14 inch deep.

airbrush–A commercial art method of painting with a fine spray to produce tonal gradations and to retouch photographs.

align–To line up letters or words on the same horizontal or vertical line.

art director–A person whose responsibilities include the selection of visual work and the talent to produce it, the purchase of visual work, and the supervision and quality and character of visual work.

bleed–Printing past the edge of the page so that when the page is trimmed, it has no margin.

blueline–A printer's proof made from negatives of the piece to be printed. It provides an opportunity to make sure all of the elements are positioned correctly before printing. Some printers call it a silver print. After the blueline has been approved, the piece is ready to be printed.

body copy–The main copy block, as distinguished from headline, subheads, coupon copy, and other elements.

boldface–Type that is heavier than type with which it is used.

bug–Identification mark usually printed in an inconspicuous area of a printed ad.

bulk mailing–Third-class mail sorted by states and cities and delivered to the post office in bundles. Third-class mail usually is the slowest and least-reliable method.

bullets–Round, solid dots that are aligned to call out information.

camera-ready art–Material given to printer that is ready for production.

character–An individual letter, figure, or other unit of type.

circulation–The number of copies of a publication distributed.

city zone–The portion of a newspaper's coverage area that includes the corporate city plus adjacent areas with the characteristics of the city.

classified advertising–Advertising arranged according to the product or service advertised and usually restricted in size and format. Display advertising in the classified section of the newspaper permits illustrations and greater variety in size and format.

clip art–Illustrations, figures, and designs that can be purchased in printed sheets for use in mechanicals of ads.

closing date–The final date on which advertising must be delivered to a medium if it is to appear in a specific issue or time slot.

color separation–The process of photographing color art or photography with filters to break them down into their primary-color components so that when the colors are combined in printing, they create the illusion of a full-color image.

column inch–A unit of publication space one column wide and 1 inch deep.

combination rate–A special rate for advertising in two or more publications under the same ownership.

comprehensive (comp)–A layout prepared to resemble the finished advertisement as closely as possible.

continuity in advertising–Repetition of the same basic theme, layout, or commercial format. In media, continuity refers to the regularity with which messages appear in an advertising medium.

continuous tone–An image that contains tones ranging from black to white in contrast to line art (see also *halftone*).

cooperative advertising–Advertising paid for or partially paid for by vendors.

copyright–Legal protection against the reprinting, use, or sale of an original work without expressed consent.

copywriter–The wordsmith of an agency who create the headlines and body copy of advertisements.

corporate advertising–Advertising that stresses the company in general rather than promoting a company's specific product or brand.

cost per thousand–The cost to the advertiser for the delivery of a message to 1,000 readers, viewers, or listeners.

coverage–The percentage of households or individuals who are exposed to a specific advertising medium in a given area.

crop–To remove portions of an illustration by trimming the edges.

crop marks–Marks along the margins of an ad or photograph indicate the portion to be reproduced.

cut–To delete portions of copy or program material to fit a particular space or time period.

deadline–The hour or day after which advertising will not be accepted for appearance in a specific edition or a publication or specific broadcast time period.

demographics–The statistical description of a market based upon such facts as age, sex, marital status, education, etc. Typical break-downs include-

Women	Men
18-24	18-24
25-34	25-34
35-49	35-49
50 and over	50 and over

display advertisements–Advertisements using attention-attracting elements (such as illustrations, photographs, and typography) in contrast to classified advertising.

double column–Pages that consist of two vertical columns of type rather than type extending across the entire page.

double page spread–An advertisement appearing on two facing pages.

double truck–Another term for a double-page spread.

dummy–A paper model indicating the size, shape, and layout of the finished printed product.

fact sheet–An outline of key product facts supplied to copywriters or the broadcast announcers, who use it as a basis for ad-libbedrather than prepared commercials.

floppy disk–A thin magnetic disk for storage of computer information.

flush–Printed matter set even with the margin, other material, or with the edge of the page.

font–A complete assortment of type in one size and typeface.

format–The size, shape, style, and appearance of a publication, printed page, or advertisement.

four-color process–A printing process that separates the color image into red, yellow, blue, and black negatives and reproduces a full range of colors by overprinting these colors from plates made from the negatives.

frequency–The number of times an advertising message is delivered within a set period of time.

graphic artist–Any visual artist working in the commercial art field.

graphic designer–A professional graphic artist who works with the elements of typography, illustration, photography, and printing. A visual problem solver.

halftone–A continuous-tone image that is photographed through a screen to break it up into tiny dots so that from normal viewing distance it appears as continuous shades or tones. The density of the dots varies with the printing method and quality desired.

illustration–A picture or diagram that helps make something clear or attractive. In advertising, several kinds of illustrations are used: including airbrush, marker, pen and ink, watercolor, and computer art. A pen and ink drawing is simply an illustration created with a pen and ink (usually a series of line work, stippling, cross-hatching, and ink washes). A watercolor illustration is produced by adding water to pigment to create a wash of color. Computer art illustrations are created using illustration software applications instead of traditional methods.

illustration board–A bristol board suitable for airbrush, pencil, pen, or watercolor. It is made with a close texture.

illustrator–A professional graphic artist who communicates a pictorial idea by using paint, pencil, pen, collage, or any other graphic technique except photography.

insertion order–Written authorization for a publication to print an advertisement of a specified size in a particular issue at a stated rate.

justify type–Arranging lines of type so that they align on both the left and right.

keying of an advertisement–Putting a code number or letter in a coupon or in the advertiser's address so that the particular advertisement or medium producing an inquiry can be identified.

kiosk–An ad display that is usually back lit. Typically seen in malls or airports.

layout–The arrangement of creative elements on a printed page: headlines, copy blocks, illustrations, logotypes, and other items. The layout serves as a blueprint for the finished ad.

linage–Any amount of advertising space measured in agate lines.

logo–The graphic used as the "signature" of an advertiser.

make good–Repeating an advertisement without charge or refunding space or time charges as compensation for an advertisement omitted or for one containing a significant error.

market–People who are prospective customers for a product or service.

matte finish–A coated paper with a dull finish without gloss or luster.

mechanical–The pasted-up type and illustration (also called the paste-up) suitable to be reproduced by the media or printer.

one-time rate–The rate paid by an advertiser who does not use enough space or time to earn volume discounts.

open rate–an advertising rate subject to discounts for volume or frequency.

paste-up (also called mechanical)–A layout in which illustrations and typeset text are combined on one sheet for reproduction as a single unit.

penetration–The ability of an advertising medium to reach a certain percentage of homes or prospects in a given geographical area.

photocomposition–A method of setting type based on photography.

photostat (or stat)–An inexpensive, but high-quality photoprint made by a camera that can generate images with or without a negative. These photoprints are often used for line art. Stats may be matte, glossy, or reversed according to the specific needs of the job.

pica–A unit of measurement for type or other printed material: 6 picas equal 1 inch.

PMS–The Pantone Color Matching System

point–The smallest typographical unit of measurement: 12 points equal 1 pica, and 72 points equal 1 inch.

preferred position–Any advertisement position in publications for which the advertiser must pay a premium when specifically ordering it.

primary colors–In printing, these colors are red, yellow, and blue.

primary market–The largest group of buyers expected to purchase homes in a community.

process printing–Printing in which one color is printed over another with transparent inks to produce different hues.

psychographics–The break down of a particular market by using attitudes, feelings, and emotions as indicators.

proof–An impression of the type and/or illustrations on paper.

publicity–A story or message about a product or a company prepared as editorial rather than advertising material and published or broadcast without cost. Publicity often results from a press release prepared by the builder or a member of the builder's staff.

run of paper (ROP)–A term that indicates that the position of an advertisement will be at the publisher's discretion.

rate card–A card listing rates for space or time, specifications for any advertisements submitted, and other data advertisers usually require.

rate holder–The minimum size advertisement that must appear in a medium during a specific period if the advertiser is to earn a frequent discount rate.

reach–The number of different homes, people, or prospects reached by one or a group of commercials or advertisements.

release–A signed statement by a person quoted or photographed to authorize use of the statement or photograph for advertising purposes.

resizing–The production of an advertisement in various sizes for different units of space.

retouching–Correcting or improving photographs or other artwork prior to printing.

reverse type–Type appearing in white on a black background.

rough–A preliminary sketch of an illustration or layout.

scanner–An electronic device used in the making of color and tone-corrected color separations.

secondary market–The second largest group of buyers expected to purchase homes in a community.

snipe–A line of text that usually appears in some sort of banner form along the top of an ad. Used to announce important information.

spec'd (specified)–Spec'd copy gives details of items such as paper, bindery techniques, type, and the like, which have been determined for a given job.

spread–Two facing pages in a publication also called a double truck.

stat–A photostat.

stet–A proofreader's term meaning to leave copy marked for corrections as is. Latin for "let it stand."

tabloid–A newspaper usually about one-half the standard size, approximately 11 ¾ inches wide and from 15 to 17 inches long.

target market–That part of the general population most likely to buy a particular product or service.

tear sheet–A page containing an advertisement torn or clipped from a publication.

teaser–Any advertisement that stimulates curiosity by limiting information while promising more information in future messages.

text–Straight type matter or body copy, as distinguished from headlines and subheads.

thumbnail–A rough layout in miniature.

transient rate–The flat or one-time rate for advertising without quality or frequency discounts.

typeface–A style or design of type encompassing shape, weight, and proportions that make it distinct from other typefaces.

typo–An error in typed copy that has been typeset or input into a computer.

typography–The art or skill of designing printed matter, especially words, using different typefaces.

velox–A black and white print of the halftone image.

vignette–An illustration in which the background fades gradually away until it blends into the unprinted paper.

widow–Part of a word, a single word, or short line of type at the end of a paragraph, particularly at the bottom of a column or page. Widows should be avoided if at all possible. Orphans are such items at the top of a column or page.

NOTES

Chapter 1. Strategy: Target Marketing

1. "Welcome to the Buyer's Market," *Builder* Magazine, July 1992, Special Issue.

Chapter 4. Fair Housing Compliance

2.-8. U.S. Department of Housing and Urban Development, *Implementation of the Fair Housing Amendment Act of 1988,* 24CFR, Section 109.30, pp. 2-7.

INCREASE YOUR PROFITS
with These Other Home Builder Press Products

Looking Good Is Good Business: A Handbook of Publicity and Promotion Techniques Every Builder Should Use–*John Bertram*–This handbook tells you how to create a positive image for your company and how to increase sales with promotional ideas that can be less expensive and more effective than paid advertising. *Looking Good* explores promotion fundamentals, including how to plan special events, get free media coverage, distribute press releases, and more. Contains sample display ads, editorial articles, newsletters, and mailers to raise community awareness of your business.

Marketing Made Easy! Basics for Home Builders–*E. Lee Reid*–This practical handbook for small-volume builders contains a wealth of ideas any builder can use to increase traffic. The mostly inexpensive marketing ideas it describes are easy for you to organize and to do. *Marketing Made Easy!* also shows you how to evaluate your current market efforts, determine your needs, create a distinct market identity, outline your goals, plan and budget for marketing, and evaluate your competition.

Selling New Homes–*Clark Parker Associates*–Improve your sales program with the practical advice this book offers on how to use new home sales techniques, sell through brokers versus in-house salespeople, compensate a sales team, develop a sales manual, and more.

Marketing Your Remodeling Services: Putting the Pieces Together–*Carol Davitt*–If you are diversifying into remodeling, this book can show you how to use professional marketing techniques without spending a lot of time and money. The easy-to-follow 10-step plan shows you how to start with inexpensive efforts and add others as time and money allow. It includes a simple marketing plan, press release, company newsletter, and more to get you started.

Selling Remodeling: Nine Steps to Sales Success–*Victoria Downing with an introduction by Linda W. Case*–Diversifying builders can learn more about how to close sales without resorting to uncomfortable high-pressure sales techniques. You can increase your business with this proven nine-step system, including how to build rapport with prospects, gather information, uncover a prospect's objections, ask for and close the sale, follow up, and more.

To order or for more information on other products or to request a catalog, call or write the Home Builder Bookstore:

Home Builder Bookstore
National Association of Home Builders
1201 15th Street, NW
Washington, DC 20005-2800
(800) 223-2665
http://www.u-web.com/builderbooks